GHOSTS

GHOSTS

Jon Izzard

spruce

Dedication

To Margaret Dolan and all the reporters at Bristol and Gloucester Crown Courts, whose commitment is rarely noticed by any save the divine patron of their craft—Thoth—recorder of judgments at the weighing of the soul. May he work some magic for us all.

Caveat

While the text and illustrations may portray ghosts in a realistic way, the author asserts that the objective reality of ghosts should not be inferred from anything stated or depicted in this work. No part of this work should be regarded as offering recommendations that should be acted upon, particularly in regard to medical conditions: always seek professional advice if you have any concerns.

An Hachette UK Company
First published in Great Britain in 2010 by
Spruce, a division of Octopus Publishing Group Ltd
Endeavour House, 189 Shaftesbury Avenue,
London, WC2H 8JY
www.octopusbooks.co.uk

Distributed in the U.S.A. and Canada for
Octopus Books USA
c/- Hachette Book Group USA
237 Park Avenue
New York, NY 10017

Copyright © Octopus Publishing Group Ltd 2010
Text copyright © Jon Izzard 2010

Jon Izzard asserts the moral right to be identified as the author of this book.

Produced by Bookworx
Editor: Jo Godfrey Wood, Designer: Peggy Sadler

ISBN-13: 978-1-84601-370-6
ISBN-10: 1-84601-370-4

A CIP catalogue record of this book is available from the British Library.

Printed and bound in China

10 9 8 7 6 5 4 3 2 1

CONTENTS

Introduction 6

Chapter 1
Ghosts: The Spirit World
10

Chapter 2
Ghosts: Echoes in Time
54

Chapter 3
Interactive Ghosts
74

Chapter 4
Ghost-hunting
116

Chapter 5
Defense Against Ghosts
158

Glossary 180   Bibliography 184
Further Reading 186   Index 188

Introduction

Life after death is the cornerstone of popular religions: from Christianity, Islam, and Judaism, to Hinduism and Buddhism. For millennia, we have been taught that we each have a soul that continues our existence long after our body is laid to eternal rest. Ghosts are part of that ancient tradition and hauntings happen when something simply interrupts the soul's passage from body to its allotted place in Heaven, Hell, Purgatory, or wherever. But while religion teaches that people have souls, what about the ghosts of animals, trees, or even entire houses? Do ghost trains and ghost ships have souls? What are ghost clothes made of—why doesn't our eternal soul roam around stark naked? Science has even more difficulty. Despite an army of paranormal researchers with an arsenal of ghost-hunting gadgets, not a single spook has been proven to exist. In fact, paranormal researchers can't even agree what a ghost is. Witnesses report such a bewildering variety of experiences, with so many gray areas, that they defied taxonomic classification. Many ghosts are spirits of the dead, but some are spirits of the living. Some ghosts seem as real as anyone of flesh and blood and can be seen, heard, smelled, and touched; while others only manifest in our dreams. Most, perhaps, visit while we are wide awake, yet we only sense them in a way that cannot be described, except to say that we know we are no longer alone.

DON'T LOOK NOW, BUT...

What if there was a ghost beside you, right now, reading over your shoulder? How would you know? And should you thrill with excitement at meeting a great mystery, or cringe in fear at the chill of its charnel breath on your neck? According to most mediums, ghosts are around us all the time and we don't need to visit a haunted house to find them. A trip down the high street means walking through them—they're in stores,

IT'S BEHIND YOU!

Kathy Kriticos (Shannon Elizabeth) is perilously unaware of the ghost of a suicide victim known as the Angry Princess (Shawna Loyer) in the movie *Thir13en Ghosts* (2001).

bars, hotels, at work. Almost everyone has had a ghostly experience or knows someone who has. Most are fleeting events that stick in our minds because we can't explain them. But ghosts are far from inconsequential; they have the power to throw us around like rag dolls, suck us into TV sets, and even destroy our minds and lives—allegedly.

OPENING OUR EYES AND MINDS

When we think about ghosts we stand at the edge of an abyss of fabulous possibilities—eternal life, reincarnation, where soul mates find each other and fall in love again and again, and new dimensions of spiritual planes inhabited by gods and devils. The imaginative mind reels at such wonders, but many people have closed their minds to the idea and believe that ghosts simply don't exist. For many, the solution to the question "Do ghosts exist?" is to find out for themselves. And often the easiest and safest way is to become part of a proper investigation team. Some of us might relish the thought of meeting ghosts mind to mind and communicating directly with the dead. Others prefer to keep them at arm's length and use hi-tech instruments to register their presence. Perhaps the most common advice shared among ghost-hunters is to expect the unexpected. We can certainly minimize the risks, but all field research into the paranormal carries an element of danger. There are techniques for protecting ourselves from attack by malevolent ghosts, ranging from simple talismans and short prayers, to complex rituals in accordance with religious teachings. It is no coincidence that religions have techniques for dealing with the unquiet dead and almost every organized religion declares that we each have an eternal soul, while many doctrines are devoted to keeping this soul healthy while we're alive; happy when we're dead. The promise of eternal reward or punishment is one of the most powerful tools of social control ever devised. And when religion is compounded with politics to wield authority over the mundane as well as the divine, it is no surprise that some spiritual empires have been vying to rule the Earth for millennia.

THE MANY KINDS OF GHOSTS

Some ghosts are like echoes or ripples through time; they show us an event in history and repeat the same actions over and over again. These ghosts may be made of the same stuff as the past itself, which has somehow leaked into the present. Or maybe the events have imprinted themselves on the very fabric of space-time like a recording that is played back periodically. But the other sort of ghosts, such as loved ones who return briefly with a message of consolation, or vengeful ghosts desperately staying Earthbound to right a wrong—what are they made of? Some people think they manifest by vampirizing energy from their surroundings (making detectable "cold spots"), or they simply exist in a region as yet unexplored by science. Such ghosts would be unrestricted in the way they look and move. They may make noises, generate odors, touch us, and move objects around. Some ideas about ghosts that have been unchallenged for millennia are now being investigated by modern science and found to be rare but natural events. Ghost-hunters need to be aware of these, to avoid arriving at false conclusions. But some mediums regard scientific interference in spiritual issues as unhelpful distraction—materialistic scientists may dissect the world into ever-smaller pieces, always missing the point. While most reports of ghostly phenomena can be explained through natural causes, the cases that remain, like ghosts themselves, will haunt us until we can lay them to rest.

SEEK AND WE SHALL FIND

One thing is strikingly clear: all ghost stories are slightly different. Some are about love affairs disrupted by tragic deaths; some have never-dying hatreds burning for revenge; some have trapped lonely spirits yearning for liberation and peace; some have moods of gloom or joy, with bursts of energy, unbearable voices in the dark night, and nerve-jangling anticipation of what's to come. All these hallmarks of the classic haunted house are exactly the same as the living contents of the human mind. The most haunted house we could possibly live in is probably ourselves.

1
Ghosts: The Spirit World

The Realm of Ghosts

SEEKING EXPLANATIONS

Strange and ghostly things happen, sometimes, to almost all of us. When they do, we sensibly seek an explanation, a reason, a cause. Many of us find ready-made solutions and interpret our experiences in the light of our religion, using explanations many centuries, even many millennia, old. Some people believe this is actually how religions began, as carefully constructed models of an unseen world created to make sense of phenomena that doesn't fit into our knowledge of the physical world.

Many of us yearn to experience something out of the ordinary, and ghosts are just one facet of the paranormal that includes UFOs, monsters, extrasensory perception, angels, and the spiritual dimensions. The realm of spirit is vast and includes angels, demons, gods, and goddesses, as well as beings that have evolved beyond their physical selves to become pure spirit. And all these can inhabit universes that co-exist with ours, but of which we are unaware in the normal course of events.

FINDING ANSWERS

Meeting a ghost can seem like a rite of passage, a first step into a larger, more profound, world, and many of us can't wait for it to happen. Perversely, this anxiety can actually inhibit our perception of the unexplained. But if we feel impatient waiting for something spooky to happen to us, we should take comfort in the fact that we are all, right now, experiencing an even greater mystery: the process of creation. While some of us take creation stories literally, others say they are merely metaphors. But even modern science is lost in a confusion of exotic theories when it comes to answering the most fundamental question—how does anything exist at all?

Ghosts—the undying spirits of human beings—have journeyed into a realm beyond the physical world and have gained a unique insight into the mysteries of life and death. If we could contact them, surely they would teach us at least some of the ultimate secrets. But, apart from communicating the idea that it's generally worth keeping ourselves alive and searching for the answers, replies from the spirit world seem to be either vague and veiled, or are mundane messages from loved ones urging us to cheer up—we'll meet again later.

THE QUEST FOR ORDER IN CHAOS

If the ghosts themselves cannot give us answers, studying their behavior should help us to work it out for ourselves. As we sift through these clues, we find a very wide range of experiences are lumped together under the umbrella term "ghost." No definitive breakdown into discrete classifications has yet been comprehensively agreed, but there are some major groups that exhibit unique points of interest.

The classic haunting

This is the consciousness of a person that has survived their death and it can interact with the witnesses. Whether it is actually the person's soul or spirit is a moot point, but this manifestation possesses all the memories and personality of the deceased. A good example would be a "crisis apparition" (see page 20), where the figure of the person is seen unexpectedly and they inform you that they have just died. Mediums allegedly communicate with these spirits.

The location-based ghost

A scene from the past is replayed time after time, in exactly the same way, and at exactly the same place. These ghosts show no awareness of present-day witnesses and may include, or even consist of, inanimate objects such as trains, planes, and houses.

A battlefield haunted by the sights and sounds of the original conflict is a typical example of this sort of manifestation (see pages 56–9), also known as a "residual" energy haunting, a "stone-tape recording," an echo, a shadow, or revenant.

Ghosts of the living

Similar to the crisis apparition, the spirit of a living person is sometimes seen, often going through a crisis situation, but one that the person survives. Many near-death experiences fall into this category. The arrival apparition, in which somebody is seen at a place before they have physically arrived there, is a very common example (see page 21). These cases often exhibit some similarities with poltergeists.

Poltergeists

Some researchers think most, if not all, poltergeist phenomena is caused by living people, but without them knowing it, as the latent power of the mind erupts into events such as moving objects. While poltergeists are often reported as ghosts, these powers are linked with the inert but powerful energy allegedly consciously manipulated in witchcraft and a host of other magical rituals.

Pure spirits

These are spirits that never inhabited a physical body, human or otherwise. Angels, demons, gods, and goddesses all belong to this group, as may some nature spirits such as fairies.

Earth mysteries

Rare but perfectly natural events, such as ball lightning, or electromagnetic and infrasound phenomena associated with earthquakes, may give rise to reports of ghostly events such as weirdly glowing lights and powerful feelings of a paranormal presence.

Hoaxes and delusion

While not especially common, hoaxes do occur and this is one reason why many vigils are held in secret—to prevent pranksters creating false phenomena. People who are suffering from certain mental illnesses or using drugs are prone to hallucinations and may easily misinterpret a perfectly natural event in a supernatural way. In addition, ordinary tiredness can also replicate some of these aberrations, incorporating dreamlike episodes.

The Human Spirit

First let us consider the human spirit itself, the soul—that mysterious element at the core of each of us that may have the potential to become Earthbound as a ghost.

When someone dies a peaceful death the most obvious sign is that the body stops breathing—with the final exhalation, life departs. So it is a short leap of faith to believe that the life that inhabited the body left in that breath and it is no surprise the Latin word for breath—*spiritus*—gives us our word "spirit." Millennia ago, the observation that the soul was an invisible, intangible vapor would have been leading-edge science. However, answers always seem to generate more questions. Did this spirit stay around us, or, like the smoke from a pyre, ascend to the heavens? What are its limits, its powers, and its destiny? If it returns to this world is it, in fact, a ghost?

HUMAN STATES

The permanent departure of the soul brings death to the body, but it seems that the human spirit may sometimes leave temporarily and return—sometimes without the person even being aware of it—for example, when we are asleep or in a near-sleep state.

The significance of dreams

Each night, when we explore strange and fascinating lands in our dreams, some people say that our spirit is out of our body and traveling through the so-called astral planes. The sensation can be powerful, particularly during our lucid dreaming periods—when we actually realize that we're dreaming and in control of our actions, but remain in the dream world.

Near-sleep trance states

Sometimes, it is claimed, the spirit may travel around the landscape of the waking world. While this may occur during sleep or when we are on the verge of sleep, some people claim to be able to put themselves into a sort of trance and consciously allow their spirit to leave their body.

The potential value of such excursions has not been ignored by the military, who have actually investigated the possibility of using this ability for remote viewing—spying by sending the spirit, or astral body, to a specific location where they couldn't physically go.

OUT-OF-BODY EXPERIENCE

The well-known occultist, Dr. De Sarak, is shown here in a trance at an esoteric seance, in 1908. He has been photographed in the company of his "astral double." Opinion is divided as to whether this photograph is a clever fake, such as a double exposure, or not.

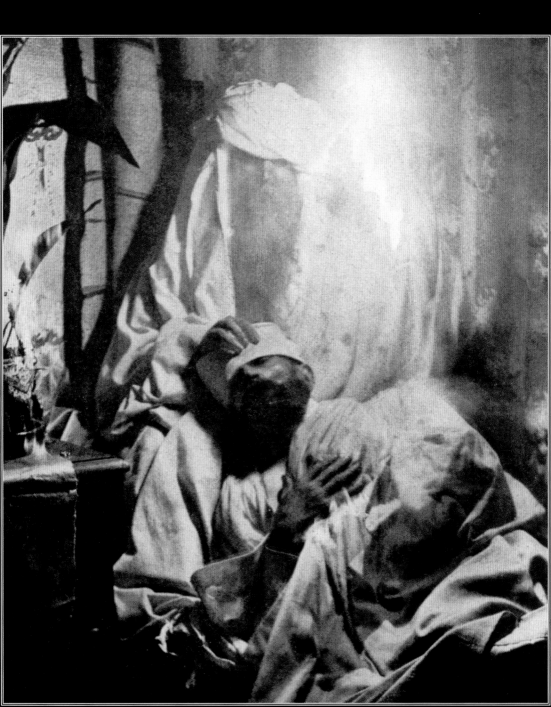

"Time travel" or precognition?

Apart from wandering the world as a spirit, some people claim to have gone back and investigated past lives; while others travel forward and return with knowledge of the future—precognition. These are extraordinary assertions, which the modern scientific community has yet to accept.

Nightmares

The nightmare is a powerful type of haunting. This is not just a "bad dream," but rather when the person wakes up and finds that their body is tightly pinned down by what they might think is a ghost. Reports of the assailant, usually unseen, vary—from medieval demons that squat on chests, squeezing the breath out, to modern cases of alleged alien abduction, where victims are paralyzed by advanced technology.

Sleep paralysis

In recent years scientific research has opened a new window into the physiology of such events. The key breakthrough came in the study of sleep paralysis; the body's natural defense against acting out dreams. In a nightmare we actually wake when our body expects us to be asleep. So, we briefly remain under the natural control of our defensive paralysis and are not able to move. Immobilized, we make the natural assumption that the event is actually an attack on us. If we are already feeling threatened by a haunting, as we are so close to sleep, we may conjure a vivid image of a ghost assaulting us.

DAYDREAMING AND VISIONS

Some ghostly episodes may take place in the blink of an eye, when we lapse into a daydreaming state. While the dialog may now seem somewhat dated in the 1946 romantic movie *Stairway to Heaven* (see pages 18–19), the theme has an eternal quality.

Peter, a young man, misses his appointment with death and falls in love. He is visited by a ghost who has come to collect his soul, but he refuses to give it up, explaining that he now has everything to live for—his new love. Assuming that the visitor is a hallucination brought about by a brain disorder, he undergoes surgery, during which his soul faces a trial. In a moving study of human nature, the trial weighs his soul for the right to live as he chooses.

Glimpses of the Afterlife

Many real-life visions of the portal to the Afterlife describe the light as shining with love and being the best thing the person has ever encountered. Sometimes the spirits of ancestors or loved ones appear in the light, beckoning reassuringly. The welcoming spirit may even be their favorite deceased screen or music idol.

Seeing Himself

An anonymous Irish author, writing in the 9th century CE, tells of a religious student who bumps his head on a lintel and falls unconscious. His spirit sees his body on the ground but fails to recognize it. The spirit goes to fetch a priest, but the priest cannot see him and neither can anyone else.

REALIZATION
In great distress he runs from person to person, but no one can see or hear him. His body is soon discovered and carried to the graveyard. Here the spirit finally realizes that the body is in fact his own. Then the spirit of his dead brother comes to him and tells him that he must return to his body.

The man is terrified and overcome with loathing at the thought of entering what looks like a corpse. But the dead brother insists that he must do this. And so he does, and lives for a full year thereafter.

A NEAR-DEATH EXPERIENCE

While some people may experience voluntary projection of their spirit, most exteriorizations are involuntary, in sleep. But sleep isn't the only portal through which the spirit may voyage.

In 1988 actress Jane Seymour was filming a TV mini-series in Madrid, Spain (*Onassis: The Richest Man in the World*), when she was given an injection of antibiotics.

She suffered a severe anaphylactic shock and found herself outside of her body. From the corner of her room, she looked down at the medics' desperate efforts to resuscitate her. She felt no pain and was rational, puzzled because she knew it was her down there, yet here she was, separate from her body. She felt that she must be dying, but she didn't feel ready to leave everything behind and fervently wished that she could stay to look after her children and do so much more in the world. The next thing she knew she was back in her body, being treated and saved from possible death.

Her experience is typical of people who claim to have experienced an involuntary projection of their spirit during a sudden trauma.

STAIRWAY TO HEAVEN →

In the movie *Stairway to Heaven*, made in 1946, David Niven (1909–1983), the British leading man, is hallucinating while he is having an operation performed on his brain and his ghostly imaginings are viewed in this scene.

Crisis Apparitions

 A "crisis apparition" is one in which the ghost visits those with whom they enjoyed a special bond when they were alive. Mostly they occur at night, in our dreams, or when a sudden awakening reveals the spirit at the foot of our bed. In these instances, although we may feel wide awake, we may be in what is known as the "hypnagogic state," the transition between sleep and wakefulness. At this time the boundary between dream hallucinations and ordinary sight is blurred. Some people say this is a state in which we can see the spirit world more clearly.

A TRUE STORY

The following true story illustrates this phenomenon. One New Year's Eve, 18-year-old Jacqui Stavrinou was getting ready to go out with friends and popped downstairs to fetch something.

"On opening the door I looked across the room and there, on my couch, was Uncle Jim. I looked at him for a moment, as I was very surprised to see him there. He was a tall gent and always very smartly dressed, even at home. I reached for the light switch and looked again, but he was gone. I really didn't think much more about it and went out for the evening. The next day I met up with my sister. The first thing she did was pull me to one side. I just looked at her and said 'I know, Uncle Jim passed away last night didn't he? About 7.45 p.m.' She looked shocked, I was right—he had passed away just before I had seen him. It always brings me comfort to know that he visited me."

The popular British author Henry Rider Haggard had a troubled dream in which he was visited by Bob, a dog. At around 2 a.m. on Sunday 10 July 1904 he dreamed of the black retriever dog, which was lying in brushwood by water, with its head at an unnatural angle. Bob was trying to speak in words the man could understand and although he couldn't achieve this, it was clear Bob was dying.

The dreamer's wife was so alarmed by the weird noises her husband was making in his sleep, she woke him from this terrible dream. They investigated and found the body of the dog in a place as described. He had been knocked down and instantly killed by a train at around 10.35 p.m. the previous evening. The time difference between the death and the dream is not easy to explain, but perhaps Bob simply couldn't get his message through until Haggard was in the right phase of dreaming sleep.

Arrival Apparitions

 Arrival apparitions are ghosts of living people who may be seen, heard, and even smelled, as if they are physically present. They are often known by their Norwegian name of *vardoger*, or "forerunner." Unlike crisis apparitions, these projections occur in situations of little or no stress. Another common feature is that the person whose apparition is seen has no conscious experience of bi-location.

MARK TWAIN'S STORY

One of the most famous examples of this phenomenon occurred to the American author Mark Twain. He was attending a crowded reception at the Windsor Hotel, Montreal, and at around 2 p.m. he noticed a woman arriving who he hadn't seen in 20 years. He wasn't expecting her and hadn't given her any thought for years, but was delighted to see her.

He was impatient for her to filter through the throng to speak with him. He saw her fully and clearly and noted the details of how she was dressed during the several times he caught sight of her. But to his great disappointment she failed to reach him. That evening, as he arrived at a lecture hall, he was taken aside to a waiting room, where, he was assured, he would recognize a friend.

And there, among ten women, was his friend. She was dressed exactly as before and he instantly addressed her warmly and declared that he had seen her at the reception.

To his astonishment she told him that she'd only just arrived by train from Quebec. He came to the conclusion the experience was created by some sort of telepathy—"mental telegraphy," as he called it.

A CHILD'S STORY

On another occasion, when Kai Taylor was a child, he greeted his father with this story on his return from work:

"I was at the computer in the lounge and I heard you come home. I said 'hello' and then I saw you walk into the kitchen. I thought you were there to drop stuff off, unload, and I went to help you, but you weren't there! Five minutes later you came home."

The incident occurred around 12.30 in the afternoon, when the father was nearly half a mile away, walking home. He didn't recall being particularly impatient to be home or thinking about what he'd do when he arrived, but there were no further stops along the way—he was heading directly home.

Ghostly Phenomena

Watching movies about ghosts and reading books about them can both be spine-chilling experiences, though filmed versions of novels can sometimes be disappointing as they are often sensationalized. Even without this bias, we are all spiritual beings and everyone has their own experience of what this means, so it can be difficult to tell what is what in the spirit world. How can we tell what is a ghost, a demon, an angel, or just a trick of the eye? Our own interpretation is everything.

GHOSTS AND DEMONS

A malevolent ghost can easily be mistaken for a demon, and vice versa, because their behavior is so similar. In the movie world the biggest haunted house feature of 2009 was *Paranormal Activity* (see pages 24–5). Initially the spirit causing the activity was assumed to be a ghost, but audiences who weren't already hiding behind their cinema seats soon discovered it was a spirit of a different complexion. *Paranormal Activity* is really about a demon, like the infamous 1979 movie *The Amityville Horror* (allegedly based on true events,) so, strictly speaking, the movie that wins the ghost story prize is probably *The Haunting in Connecticut* (see pages 26–7), although even that was based on events with a demonic slant.

GHOSTS AND ANGELS

Demons are not the only spiritual entities that may be mistaken for ghosts. Angels are spiritual messengers, and they too may manifest in a way

UNDER AN ANGEL'S WING

Sometimes, when our strength and hope are exhausted, help and comfort may arrive to support and protect us—this may be seen as a guardian angel, as in this illustration from 1914.

An Experience of a Presence

This is a typical example of a common haunting, usually known as a "presence." The following true event happened to a young person one summer.

"It was the summer of 1976 and I had finished with formal education earlier that year. Following a stint as a field archeologist, I found myself loafing with art students as a guest at a shared flat on the English Riviera at Torquay, UK. The summer seemed open-ended: an idyllic round of late rising, glorious afternoons basking in the sun, and evenings spent sampling the nightlife in this world-famous seaside resort. While the others were out one morning, I was sitting comfortably in the lounge, browsing a book on art history. I began to feel I was no longer alone. My eyes were inexorably drawn to an armchair a short distance away, as if someone were sitting there—someone who could not be ignored.

"I received a clear mental impression of a softly glowing orb of light (not hard like a pearl, but diffuse, being simply more concentrated at its heart.) But this was not physical light that was shining all around—I was bathing in radiant joy, infusing me with comfort, peace, optimism, security, and trust.

"Eventually the source begin to fade away as if the space between it and me was becoming opaque. I was left with the strong impression that the source would not only continue to exist, but had existed for an indefinite time before revealing itself to me.

"Perhaps because of its location, in the closest chair and practically facing me, I assumed the visitation was for my personal benefit, although I felt sure that had somebody walked past outside, they would have had their spirits inexplicably lifted."

that makes them essentially indistinguishable from benevolent ghosts, such as spirit guides— friends or relations that watch over and protect us. These experiences are, by their nature, intimate. And many of us have felt a guiding or helping hand from a spirit wiser than ourselves at least once in our lives.

Many of us have a set of beliefs that automatically accommodate such experiences in a particular way. Some might immediately claim the example described above (see box) is a visit by a guardian angel, while others would claim it was the spirit of a protective relative, and perhaps a few might propose it was a visit from an alien from another dimension. But perhaps we should try not to pigeonhole these things. Such memorable events do not go stale and mulling over them at leisure enables us to explore possible explanations without fear or favor. In one sense, though, the visitor was literally an angel. If the word "angel" means messenger, whatever the true origin of the presence, it brought a message that some things in life cannot be instantly understood.

Paranormal Activity, the Movie

 Paranormal Activity is a remarkable movie on several levels, not least because of its position as a piece of movie history. It was created on a budget of just $15,000 and was only screened at a couple of film festivals in 2007 and 2008, until popular demand led to its widescale release in 2009, when it grossed $7 million in its first weekend.

UNEXPLAINED MOVEMENTS

Seeing the film is a little like watching a sophisticated home movie, which documents a growing catalog of phenomena occurring to a young couple: Katie (Katie Featherston) and Micah (Micah Sloat) living in a modern suburban home. The trauma begins with banging noises, keys being moved from where they were left, and doors opening and closing. All of these occurrences might be described as mild poltergeist phenomena.

The movie vividly explores the wide area of overlap between ghosts and demons. Both are invisible denizens of the spirit world, and each may communicate through a Ouija board (see pages 138–9) and EVP (Electronic Voice Phenomenon), create a wind inside a house whose doors and windows are closed, leave cryptic messages in a dusting of powder laid out for the purpose, touch people and, ultimately, even possess a human host. The final scenes demonstrate a psychokinetic power that goes toward the higher range of poltergeist activity associated with the most malevolent ghosts (although nowhere near the extremes of the 1999 version of *The Haunting*, where the house itself comes alive.)

MASQUERADING AS A DEMON

It is possible to believe in ghosts but not in demons, which are part of a spiritual hierarchy ranging from evil on one side to good on the other.

Just as an atheist might choose not to believe in God or the Devil, yet still believe in paranormal phenomena such as certain types of ghost, it is just possible that Katie and Micah were actually haunted by a long-dead, particularly nasty ghost, who tricked them into believing it was demonic. A powerful ghost intent on harm could masquerade as a demon simply to heighten the fear factor and undermine the sanity of its victim.

The opposite idea has also been proposed: the notion that ghosts are really demons intent on deluding us was particularly popular with the medieval Church.

3:08:26 AM

PARANORMAL ACTIVITY

Our minds are probably most suggestible around
3 a.m., but sometimes when things go bump in the
night there really is something to sit up and take
notice of. Capturing activity with a video camera, as
was done in this movie, is a sensible way to discover
what's going on.

The Haunting in Connecticut, the Movie

 The old adage that many a tale grows in the telling is never more true than in the movies. The 2009 movie, *The Haunting in Connecticut*, claims to be based on a true story and tells the harrowing tale of a young man, Matt Campbell (played by Kyle Gallner), who suffers from cancer.

Matt's medication can cause hallucinations and when the family moves to a new home, just as his treatment commences, he attributes his moodiness and spooky visions to the drugs. However, the house used to be a funeral parlor, and the original owner had dabbled in necromancy, using his clairvoyant son as a medium.

A DRAMATIC CONCLUSION

The movie concludes in dramatic style with the discovery that instead of being buried, bodies of the dead were stockpiled in the funeral parlor, to be used in terrible occult experiments. With their plight revealed and the prospect of decent burial at hand, the spirits are finally released from their long captivity in the house.

The story the movie claims to tell is that of the Snedeker family, who move into a house in Southington, Connecticut, in 1986. While many of the details are reasonably close to the story the Snedekers tell, no bodies are found and neither is there any child medium.

HORRIFIC HAPPENINGS

Phenomena in the Snedeker household includes mysterious voices being heard and lights being seen, objects moving and disappearing on their own, water turning to blood, and people being beaten and sexually abused by invisible entities. Weird figures are also seen, including a gaunt man with long black hair and black eyes, and another man with white hair and white eyes.

An exorcism is said to have cleared the house of evil spirits and the property has been calm for many years.

EXAGGERATION

Some researchers have suggested the core events become exaggerated out of all proportion, to the point where the story becomes a hoax.

Where potentially lucrative book and movie deals are involved, it is always sensible for the reader and audience to entertain a mild scepticism.

THE HAUNTING IN CONNECTICUT

Irrespective of whether weird phenomena are explained as ghostly manifestations or simply as a chemical imbalance in the brain, their effects can be profoundly upsetting to all concerned, as in this spine-chilling movie.

well of St. Clether, Cornwall, UK, several times, and on the third occasion (10 July 2007) she experienced a remarkable vision— apparently featuring both a ghost and a spirit.

Nature spirit

This ancient sacred site is on Bodmin Moor and is unusual not only in that there is a well house beside the chapel, but that the water flows from the well into the chapel, running beneath the granite altar itself.

To the right of the altar, Christine saw the ghost of a monk, who was the site's guardian in the Christian ministry. To the left, however, she saw a more ancient being, an elemental nature spirit from the pagan era. Here she explains it in her own words:

"On the night of the investigation I became aware of a tall, female guardian's presence to the left of the chapel's altar. It was the same guardian that I had sensed by the holy well, but instead of appearing as a transparent, green, shapeless, elemental energy, her image was quite different. Initially her appearance was of a female, with long, dark hair, wearing a green, flowing dress. She gave her name as Brigida.

"What I had thought was hair became swooping flocks of dark-colored birds. Her dress became the swaying movement of fluttering butterflies, ladybirds, bees, and leaves. There was a psychic scent of pollen, sweet roses, and pungent herbs. All these came together and formed the image that became Brigida."

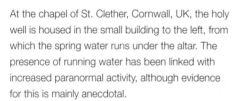

ST. CLETHER

At the chapel of St. Clether, Cornwall, UK, the holy well is housed in the small building to the left, from which the spring water runs under the altar. The presence of running water has been linked with increased paranormal activity, although evidence for this is mainly anecdotal.

GHOST AND SPIRITS

The difference between ghosts and other sorts of spirits can easily become blurred, but sometimes they are quite distinct and stand side by side. Christine Donnelly, a member of a paranormal investigation team, visited the chapel and holy

Composite divinity

Such composite divinities are not unusual; most goddesses can choose to manifest in a variety of guises. However, Christine's highly detailed vision is not commonplace, and its triple combination of visual image with scent and a name is particularly rare. Her experience was so moving that she now wears a tattoo especially commissioned to commemorate the event.

The embodiment of an idea

While we may accept the monk as the living ghost of a spiritually evolved Christian who elected to remain Earthbound, offering protection to the site and benediction to those who visit with a pure heart, we may perhaps wonder whether he too was somehow an embodiment of an idea, rather than a straightforward human spirit. Folklorists are alive to this possibility and many consider similar sightings, such as ghostly white ladies in valleys with streams or waterfalls, and green ladies in woodland glades, are likely to be visions of the genius loci—the immortal spirit of the place—and not simply the ghost of a mortal.

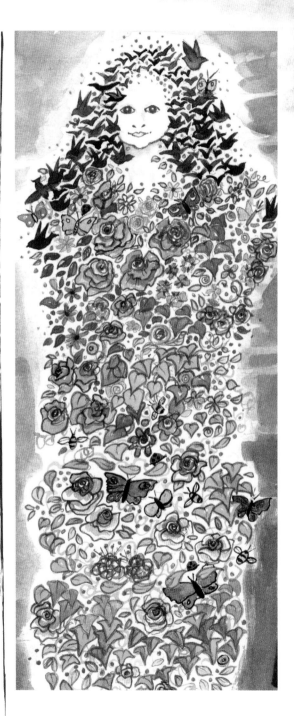

BRIGIDA

This painting by Hazel Brown was inspired by Christine Donnelly's vision, and shows the spirit's hair as a flock of birds, while her body is composed of summer flowers and colorful insects. Her presence at the well celebrates the life-giving power of water.

The Earliest Ghost Story

 The earliest-written ghost story yet found was impressed into soft, clay tablets in about 1,800 BCE, and these were copies of more ancient documents. This story was written in the language of Sumeria, using the earliest currently known writing system in the world (cuneiform) and tells of a visit to the Underworld, realm of ghosts.

When Bilgames (the Sumerian rendering of Gilgamesh) is a young man he plays with the others in the streets until, one day, his toys of willow fall down into the Underworld. He is distraught and sits at Ganzir, the gate to the Underworld, until his servant and friend Enkidu offers to go and fetch them back. Bilgames cautions Enkidu that the Underworld is a dangerous place and insists he should not draw attention to himself. He gives Enkidu a list of instructions:

- Do not wear clean clothes or they will know you're not one of them.
- Do not wear sweet perfume or they will be attracted to the scent.
- Do not throw a stick or those you hit will surround you.
- Do not take a staff of cornel wood or it will make the ghosts tremble.
- Do not wear sandals or the noise they make will shake the Underworld.

- Don't kiss a wife or son you love or hit a wife or son you hate—the uproar will capture you.

But Enkidu ignores this wise advice. He breaks every taboo and is taken before the Queen of the Underworld—Ereshkigal—who weeps constantly for her dead son, Ninazu, for whose sake she perpetually tears at her bare breasts with her fingernails and pulls out her hair. After seven days Bilgames despairs of waiting for his friend at the Gate of Ganzir and seeks assistance from the gods. Enki, wisest of all, instructs Utu, the Sun God, to help. Accordingly, as Utu rises at dawn, he makes a hole in the Underworld and brings Enkidu out.

Enkidu describes the condition of the ghosts he encounters in the Underworld. Their wellbeing generally depends on how many sons (heirs) they have—because sons give sacrifices to their ancestors' spirits and these benefit the dead. The more sons, the more offerings they receive. Those with seven sons are honored and enthroned among the lesser gods, while those with none are downcast and the only bread they have to eat is brick-hard. But there are exceptions: for example, a stillborn babe is given an afterlife sweet with milk and honey.

Enkidu mentions the fate of people who have died by various means. One who was eaten by lions still screams in agony; one who fell from a

rooftop still cannot mend his broken bones; one who died in battle lies with his head cradled by his parents accompanied by his weeping wife. There are no ghosts in the city of the Underworld who have been consumed by fire, for they had become smoke. Bilgames is so stricken by the reliance of the ghosts on offerings made by the living, that he immediately abandons his playful pastimes. He sets off with Enkidu on an adventure that, he hopes, will bring him such glory that his name is honored forever and this ghost will never be forgotten, to starve of neglect in the Underworld.

GILGAMESH

This carving depicts Gilgamesh between two bull-men, supporting a winged sun-disk. It was found in Kapara's palace at Tell-Halaf, Syria, and dates to the 9th century BCE. The sun's "death" at sunset and "birth" at dawn made it a symbol of the eternal soul, its wings allowing it to fly through the heavens.

Old Souls

Some theologians argue that the soul is a part of god, and has no taint of human personality, but many others see the soul as simply the eternal part of a person, and just another word for ghost. Concern over what happens to our loved ones after death is not a new phenomenon, and the desire to do all we can to help them is often demonstrated in ways that leave traces lasting for centuries or even millennia. Archeologists can only speculate about the rich variety of prehistoric grave goods, such as food, jewelry, and weapons, which have been found in tombs worldwide. While the tombs of kings may boast riches almost beyond measure, the writings of Ancient Egypt can also reveal precious insights into the shady world of ghosts.

EGYPTIAN BOOK OF THE DEAD

Much of the daily life of a pharaoh was governed by ritual, and his soul's journey into the Afterlife was also carefully managed. The earliest of Egypt's Pyramid Texts is to be found on the internal walls of the sepulchral pyramid of the 5th Dynasty pharaoh Unas, who died around 2,350 BCE. Our translations of these cryptic texts describe how the soul of the pharaoh ascends into the heavens. The hieroglyphs record incantations or spells of rebirth that support the pharaoh's soul in every aspect of his travels through the crucial first night. They magically give him all the things he could need such as food, drink, and strength in his spirit limbs. The spells also warn him of dangers and advise how potentially fatal perils are overcome. Many gods are invoked to assist the soul of the pharaoh, including the God of the Underworld, Osiris. The pharaoh's soul eventually wins through and enters into the presence of the Creator God, Re, and resides with him forever, riding in the boat of the Sun through the heavens.

The Afterlife for all

Later in Egypt's history, the Afterlife was democratized so all could aspire to an eternal paradise. The religious context also evolved, and Re was replaced by Osiris as the preferred partner in the Afterlife. The spells were no longer written on pyramid walls but on papyrus scrolls, and one such belonged to Ani, a high-ranking accountant. He died around 1,250 BCE, and the Papyrus of Ani is a complete version of the *Egyptian Book of the Dead*, or *Spells for Coming Forth by Day*, as it was originally called.

The spirit still endured an arduous voyage through the night, facing perilous trials that the spells could overcome. But the crux of the journey was the weighing of their soul against the feather of truth, emblem of the goddess Ma'at. The result was recorded by the god Thoth, and the honest soul would continue toward the gods, while a soul weighed down by deceit was devoured by Ammit, a demon—part lion, part hippopotamus, and part crocodile. The pure soul

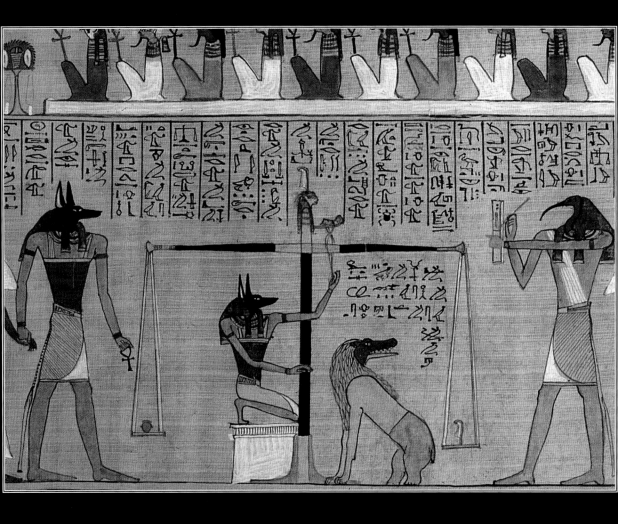

WEIGHING OF THE HEART CEREMONY

Dressed in white, the dead man watches as his heart is weighed against the Feather of Truth. If his heart is heavy with sin it will be eaten by the crocodile-headed monster Ammit, destroying all hope of entering the Afterlife. From the *Book of the Dead* of the scribe Hunefer, c.1,300 BCE.

would eventually emerge triumphantly at dawn as an immortal being to dwell with Osiris, God of the Underworld.

HADES

It is fascinating to study how ideas about the geography of the Afterlife arose in different cultures, as it can tell us a lot about their view of ghosts—and it's interesting to compare with our own. In Ancient Greece generations of visionaries contributed ideas to the mythology of the Underworld, and so the description of the realm of Hades (the Unseen) evolved. The boundary between this life and the Afterlife is generally described as a river, and the most famous image of this invokes the ferryman, Charon, who transports the souls into death. The widespread rite of putting a coin in the mouth (or on the eyes) of the recently deceased was devoutly performed so that the soul could pay for this essential passage across the River Acheron.

A gloomy landscape

One of the earliest accounts of the Underworld Erebus (Dark Shadow) is found in the *Odyssey*

THE FERRYMAN CHARON

Charon, the ferryman of the Styx, refuses to carry anyone who doesn't pay the fare; those who arrive without the necessary coin are left to gibber on the bank. Here, the ghosts are wrapped in their shrouds, the sheets in which their bodies were buried.

(see page 97), where it is described as gloomy throughout, as its name suggests. It is no wonder, then, that when the god Hermes whisks away some freshly slain ghosts on their journey to the land of the dead, that they gibber and whine, squealing like bats in a cave. The uniformly sombre landscape described by Homer eventually split into several discrete zones. The Asphodel Meadow remained as the entrance to the Underworld, and from here the soul would travel to the palace of Hades and Persephone, where they were judged by the ghosts of three mortals: Minos, Rhadamanthus, and Aeacus. Their task was to decide whether the soul should receive reward or punishment, and therefore to which zone they should be allocated.

SOCRATES

The Greek philosopher Socrates believed the soul was naked when it came to be judged, so any sins engrained in it could be seen clearly. Also, because justice needs to be seen to be done, the souls of the judges were also naked. Three paths led from this place of judgment. Sometimes the ghost would retrace its steps to the Asphodel Meadow. This would be the final resting place of those who were neither terribly bad, nor thoroughly good. It was a nondescript place, where the undistinguished dwelt.

Spirits of the unjust and evil were sent to Tartarus, the place of punishment, pain, and torment. Sometimes their suffering would enable them to overcome their sins, but other souls were set up as examples and their agonies were without end. The souls of the good, the just, the valiant, and

Visiting the Roman Underworld

 Artists through the millennia have yearned to follow a departing spirit and explore the Afterlife, yet live to return and tell their tale. The Roman poet Virgil describes the fate of the human soul in his epic poem the *Aeneid*. He also offers us the location of an entrance to the Underworld—a cave hidden beside the crater Lake Avernus, southwest Italy.

The hero, Aeneas, wishes to converse with his deceased father and consults a Sibyl for advice. This prophetess of the god Apollo explains that the way into Hades is open to all. The problem, she says, is getting back out. But Aeneas obtains the token—a plant with stem and leaves of gold that grows in the dense canopy of a holm oak tree deep in a dark valley. That night Aeneas participates in the blood-letting and burning of four sacrificial bulls, a black lamb, and a barren cow. They enter the cavern and follow the path to the River Styx. Here crowd the souls who have failed to receive a burial, each doomed to wait for a hundred years before Charon, the ferryman, will allow them across.

THE GOLDEN BOUGH

Charon is shown the Golden Bough and he conveys Aeneas and the Sybil across. On the far side, they journey past comfortless ghosts of wailing infants, miserable suicides, and broken-hearted lovers, until they arrive at a fork. The left-hand path leads to Tartarus, where the evil dead are tortured; but Aeneas's father dwells to the right, in Elysium. Here, among the meadows and groves of scented bay trees, in a valley, we find the River Lethe (Forgetfulness) and throngs of souls cluster around it. These are people who have been purged of all wrongs and have perfected their souls and enjoyed the Elysian Fields for a thousand years. Now they will drink the waters of the Lethe, which will drain them of all memory, and they will re-enter bodily life—born again, as new.

At length, when his father has told him all he needs to know, Aeneas and the Sybil leave the realm of Pluto through the Gate of Ivory. These gates offer dreamers visions of illusion and truth. Virgil does not mention it, but, as early as the 4th century BCE, devotees of the Orphic mystery religion believed there was another pool, further on from the waters of Lethe. Initiates of the cult of Orpheus believed they could escape the round of reincarnation by drinking of the pool of Mnemosyne (Memory), whose waters give the drinker's soul divine clarity. With this fully awakened consciousness, the enlightened soul may reside in Elysium forever.

Karma Law

 Belief in reincarnation often goes against the idea that all are born equal, because the spirit or ghost carries its burden of good or evil with it when it enters a baby's body. It would be surprising if we didn't ever think we might be reborn and the concept of karma is perhaps a way of explaining this. Karma is the "cause and effect" Hindu and Buddhist principle, which says that seemingly random events can be interpreted as meaningful in terms of karma, such as benefitting from, or suffering from, deeds in a previous incarnation. Such notions form a significant part of many people's personal morality. But, as the case of the reincarnated hero (see below) eventually reveals, genetics is random, so the reborn hero is never exactly the same as his ancestor. Before photographs and realistic portraits, the differences would be easy to overlook, but eventually an explanation would be needed. Increasingly complex attempts were made to understand these discrepancies. For instance, perhaps only part of the ancestor's spirit was reincarnated in him, saving the rest for another child.

If a hero's prowess could be carried forward, what about wickedness? Just as the gods might continue to favor a hero, they might punish the wicked for deeds in previous lives. In an instant, karma is born—in which deeds inevitably bring about effects. Good ones store up good karma for the future, while bad ones create a karmic debt that will need to be repaid by suffering in another life.

the heroic were sent to the Islands of the Blessed, where, as the name suggests, they dwelt in perpetual joy in the Elysian Fields.

REINCARNATION

If reincarnation is true, then everyone we know is possessed by ghosts of people long since dead, and so are we. As a basic idea, in which the soul of a person who has died is reborn in a baby's new body, reincarnation is appealingly simple. And the theory was, until scientific advances put forward an alternative view, a reasonable explanation for certain facts of life. A heroic warrior, for instance, might sire children before dying in battle. His genes might skip a generation and then produce a child who is physically similar to his illustrious forebear. With hair and eye color the same, and the same sturdy physique, the comparison would be unmistakable. The hero would appear to be reborn. Great deeds would be expected of such a child, who would receive the nurture and respect

Wisdom of the East

 We have focused so far on the ancestral roots of Western culture, but it is worth looking at how Indo-European ideas about the Afterlife developed in ancient India. The collection of Indian hymns known as the Rig Veda contains insights into the fate of the soul after death. Written in Sanskrit, these hymns are the product of a remarkable oral tradition that was handed down through millennia via an unbroken succession of chief priests. With the three other Vedas, these scriptures still lie at the heart of the living Hindu religion. The topic of death is mainly covered in the tenth and final book of the Rig Veda, believed to date to around 1,100 BCE.

One in particular is for the benefit of a person on the brink of death and is a final attempt to keep them alive. In verse after verse it bids the spirit that has left the body and traveled far away, to return so that the person may resume life here with the living. The first place from which the spirit is called back is the abode of Yama—the deified man who was the first to die and explore the realm of the Afterlife, which became his own kingdom. Then the elemental realms are each scoured for the traveling spirit—whether it has gone to the sky, earth, or ocean, it is called back. Or if it has traveled to the streaming light, among plants, to the Sun itself, or to the distant mountains, it is called back. Finally, it is called back from the abstract reaches of the cosmos: from the entire universe of motion, from that which is beyond the beyond, and from the very depths of time—past and future.

However, much as life was cherished as worth living, the Rig Veda was upbeat about the Afterlife. Yama's kingdom was hailed as the place to which we all progress, each by our own path. Yama is envisioned in his kingdom as seated beneath a tree with beautiful leaves. There, he sits drinking soma, a divine substance, in the company of the gods, playing his reed pipe and being adored in return with song. He is forever ready to welcome the dead into the company of their ancestors.

The dead, with any physical imperfections made whole by the funeral fire, ascend to Yama's realm, where they dwell in luxury in glorious houses of a thousand pillars. The priests offer sacrifices of soma for Yama and the ancestors to drink at their endless feast. In return, the priests supplicate them to be helpful and kind to their living descendents, including giving the gift of a long life here on Earth.

YAMA WAITS

Satyavan dies in his wife Savitri's arms. Yama, the
God of Death, captures his spirit with a magic noose
and leads him to the kingdom of the dead, but Savitri
follows them. Her devotion to her husband causes
Yama to release Satyavan's spirit, which restores him
to life. This tale is from the *Mahabharata*.

due to a returning champion. This upbringing would mold the child into the living embodiment of his ancestor, creating a self-fulfilling prophesy in which the spirit of the hero is reincarnated.

READING THE SIGNS

The example set by nature is persuasive. Each day the Sun appears, growing into the sky, shedding its light, then falling into a decline. Finally it disappears into the Earth and is gone. But then, every morning, it is reborn. And if we follow these days as they accumulate into a year, we see the pattern in the rising warmth of Spring, the mature heat of Summer, the waning strength of Autumn, and the frozen depths of Winter.

The lunar phases, with their endless cycle of waxing and waning, tell the same story of growth and decay, culminating in disappearance and rebirth. Finding this same pattern repeating, it's no wonder that we begin to wonder whether it could apply to our own pattern of birth, life and death, and resurrection.

Soul mates

But it is not only the rewards and punishments that might follow the immortal soul through its possibly endless journey of lives. The same idea informs us that the love between two souls may be interrupted by death, but not necessarily ended. Lovers whose souls match so perfectly that they seem to fuse into unity, could meet again, generation after generation. With each incarnation they could renew their love, transforming their lives and perfecting themselves. They may grow up actively searching for each other, instinctively knowing their other half is somewhere in the world, searching for them. And they will do all they humanly can to find each other.

Chain of incarnation

A long cycle of reincarnation would give all souls the opportunity to experience life from other points of view, especially if they could migrate into the bodies of other species. The purpose of this chain of incarnations might be to allow the evolving soul to see beyond the grand illusion that prevents it from realizing the truth of its divine nature. In that moment of transcendental clarity, the soul would achieve ultimate unity with the supreme deity. Given eternity to work in, all souls could achieve this cosmic illumination, at which point the entire Universe would become self-aware. Perhaps it would then begin a new, vast cycle of the same pattern.

GHOSTS IN THE BIBLE

Genesis, the first book of the *Bible*, refers to the Underworld, where the ghosts live. The name of this place is Sheol and it is first mentioned when Jacob is told his favorite son is dead—he replies that he will mourn to his death, when he will go to be with his son in Sheol. Sheol was the abode of all the dead, without distinction between them, and scholars think the early (pre-exile) conception of the Afterlife was generally positive and the inhabitants of Sheol were not uncomfortable in their eternal rest. Even so, archeologists have found grave goods buried with bodies, indicating that funerary rites gave significant benefits to the soul after death.

Multiple Souls

Ideas about the destiny of the soul vary. The traditional Bantu religion of Africa sees each human being as composed of multiple elements, each with a different role and fate. Zulu author Vusamazulu Credo Mutwa describes the Bantu beliefs. Every human, he says, is part of the ultimate god, whose being stretches to both extremities of time, the beginning and the end; and whose purpose is unknown.

THE DIVINE SOUL

The human body is linked through its mind to a soul and a self (Ena). The soul is divine and intimately connected with the omnipresent god, while the Ena is the "ghost." Credo Mutwa envisages the human soul as a sphere; a woman's soul has gauzy wings like those of a dragonfly. Within this orb are two worms—the red one is evil, the bright blue one is good—both in perpetual motion. The Ena, the self, does not exist when a baby is born, but builds over a lifetime. In shape and features it resembles the person precisely, but is mistily transparent. The Ena is not immortal, but needs nourishment to survive after death; in the form of thoughts and memories among the living, or of sacrificed animals. Such practices might be called ancestor worship—keeping links with ancestors alive.

A Bantu symbol meaning the Ena, or ghost.

The Enas rely on the goodwill of the living and are deemed the most helpless creatures in existence. In return for sustenance they intercede with the gods, bringing good luck. A person who tries living without the support of the Enas is like a tree without roots.

The training of witch doctors is intended to bring about the closest possible integration of the body, mind, soul, and Ena. This gives them supernatural powers because the soul and Ena exist in a time frame several days ahead of the mind and body, allowing them the gift of precognition. The soul of a human is halfway through a seven-stage evolutionary journey. It begins as a grass soul, develops into a tree stage, then a beast phase, and is then incarnated as a human. After its human life it is born as a reptile and then a bird, and finally becomes a star in the heavens, where it remains until it falls to the ground again as a shooting star. Then it begins its long journey once more.

Two-tier System for Souls

 Lazarus is taken by angels when he dies, to be with the righteous patriarch Abraham. When the rich man dies he goes straight into a fiery torment. Noticing that Abraham is far above him, he asks if Lazarus can bring down some water to ease his agony. Abraham points out there is a chasm between them and it cannot be crossed from either side. The rich man begs Abraham to send Lazarus to visit his (the rich man's) rich relations, so they'll be warned to mend their selfish ways. Abraham dismisses the idea, saying God has already given them the prophets, and if they don't believe them, they won't be convinced, even if someone rises from the dead. And, of course, he has a point. The world is still full of wealthy, selfish people ignoring poverty on their doorstep, utterly unconvinced by the story of Jesus rising from the dead.

Commonality

The ghost of the holy prophet Samuel (raised from the dead by the medium of Endor, see page 96) told the evil Saul they would soon be together in Sheol. This reveals the commonality of experience of the Afterlife. But this undifferentiated nature didn't last forever. Sheol, like Hades, was partitioned along moral lines: a section for the good and another for the bad. This later division is vividly described in Jesus's story of the beggar who died in destitution outside a wealthy man's home (see box above).

Physical resurrection

Christianity spawned a wide variety of evolutionary branches from this familiar starting point, not least of which is the idea of the physical resurrection of the body. This is why churchyards tend to align graves toward Jerusalem, so the dead can sit up and face Jesus at his second coming. Some sects believe the soul is judged the moment it dies, and its allotted reward or punishment is delivered immediately; while others prefer to hold all in abeyance until the final judgment. Roman Catholic doctrine includes a Purgatory, where the soul that is not wicked enough for Hell, but not pure enough for Heaven, is purged of its sins.

The Italian poet Dante wrote *Divine Comedy* in the first decades of the 14th century. Divided into three sections—Hell, Purgatory, and Heaven—people are urged to offer prayers to assist the cleansing of these suffering spirits, and the annual feasts of All Saints (All Hallows) and All Souls focus on the fate of souls in the Afterlife (see page 44).

DANTE'S INFERNO, THE MOVIE

Only about ten minutes of the 1935 movie *Dante's Inferno* depict the plight of souls in Hell, but the visual impact of the literally steamy scenes of naked souls writhing in fiery torment wowed audiences. Here in the caverns of Hell we see the souls of the newly dead arriving.

Hallowe'en

Ghosts in all their guises become the stuff of waking nightmares once a year in this popular festival of the dead—Hallowe'en.

Few words can send a shiver of excitement through us like Hallowe'en, and generations of children have been raised with a colorful annual celebration of ghosts, witches, pumpkin heads, and walking skeletons. Dressing up in scary costumes and playing tricks on grown-ups is a wonderful tradition and parading through the streets crying "trick or treat!" gives the delicious thrill of breaking social taboos.

As we grow into teenagers, though, the emphasis changes from fun to fright. Developing a sense of our own mortality, the idea of ghosts seems more real and we may go to costume parties for mutual support as we face up to what ghosts really are. We may even be overtaken with a desire to help trapped, suffering spirits to find freedom and peace. Some of us may hold private seances on this night. But why does all this activity take place on 31 October?

WHAT'S IN A NAME?

There is a clue in the name—Hallowe'en is really Hallows Eve, the evening before the Christian annual festival of All Hallows (or All Saints) Day. This feast is in honor of all the dead, who now see God face to face. It was celebrated on this date in England and Germany as early as 800, but was formally instituted throughout Northwest Europe in 835 by Gregory IV, who moved All Saints from its traditional date of 13 May.

Direct communion

Many people believe these saints have direct communion with God and that we can petition them to intercede on our behalf and help us in our lives. These saints may also help the spirits of deceased friends and relatives whose sins could consign them to Purgatory, or worse. The souls of ordinary people are purposefully remembered on All Souls' Day, 2 November.

BREAKING DOWN BARRIERS

Exclusive devotion to one religion is still widespread, but for more than a century a growing movement has tried to break down barriers between them and find common ground. Students of comparative religion note the many similarities between religious experiences, rather than emphasizing differences. And the similarity between a Christian prayer to the soul of a dead saint and a pagan prayer to the soul of a dead ancestor can be so striking as to seem identical to an observer. The correlation is compounded when we realize that the Christian festival of All Hallows coincides with the pagan festival Samhain. Perhaps it derived its association with death through an annual culling of livestock, or perhaps the sombre change of seasons was reason to fear the festival.

Celtic legends from Eire abound with mysterious meetings between mortals and gods on this date, suggesting the barrier between natural and supernatural either weakens or disappears at this time. However, much of the lore in literature about Samhain being a feast of the dead is based on discredited 19th-century speculation. Even so, the sheer visceral power of the turning season is enough to induce anyone to believe communion with ghosts is easier at this time of year.

JACK-O'-LANTERNS

Hollowed-out pumpkins sporting frightening human faces and other patterns adorn this richly-decorated café porch on Hallowe'en. Tradition has it that only by "trick-or-treaters."

The Day of the Dead

In contrast to the fear-haunted night of Hallowe'en, the celebration of El Día de los Muertos—the Day of the Dead—in Mexico enjoys a jovial party atmosphere. This supremely lively approach to the All Souls festival is the product of a pre-colonial, native religious festival that has integrated with the imposed Spanish creed of Roman Catholicism. It is a celebration of the intimate relationship between the living and the ghosts of their family dead, a relationship that has endured for countless generations. The indigenous festival occurred in July and August, and was a welcoming home of the souls of ancestors who lived for the rest of the year in Mictlan, the Aztec Underworld. The living would honor their ancestors by placing offerings such as gifts of food, drinks, and lights on their tombs, and telling stories of the dead, keeping their memories alive.

Ways of dying

Depending on how a person died, their soul would go to one of five destinations. Babies, for example, would go to one of the highest of 13 levels of heaven—a place of comfort and perpetual nurture, where the souls of a future race of mankind were generated. Warriors who died in battle went to the East to live with the Sun God, and enjoyed an Afterlife of song and glory. Sacrificial victims also went here. After four years, these souls might return to life as exotic birds, such as the hummingbird.

North, South, East, or West?

Women who died in childbirth went to the West, and they too might return to the realm of the living, but as spirits of ill omen. Those who died through the agency of water, either directly through drowning or indirectly through the effects of storm (including death by lightning strike) would go to the South, where they enjoyed abundance and feasting. The North was the fate of everyone else. Here, souls faced a difficult and dangerous journey through eight levels of the Underworld before they finally reached their destination at the lowest, ninth level. This journey would take four years.

The ninth level of Mictlan was a place of darkness, quietude, and rest, where its lord and lady, Mictlantecuhtli and Mictecacihuatl, lived in a windowless house. The dead were often buried with charms that would help them negotiate the hazards of the journey, as well as gifts for the

> ### DAY OF THE DEAD →
>
> The Day of the Dead holiday, celebrated in Mexico and by Latin Americans living in the USA and Canada, focuses on family and friends remembering those who have died. Some visit the graves and take the favorite foods of the dead as gifts.

Tomb-sweeping Day

 China has a long tradition of ancestor worship, and an annual cleaning of the ancestral graves is called Tomb-sweeping Day. It is part of the festival of Pure Brightness (Qingming), which is held on the 15th day after the spring equinox (i.e. on the 4th or 5th of April), and which celebrates the return of Spring, welcoming the warmer weather, and giving free rein to natural enthusiasm for life.

The graves are not only tidied, but people also make offerings of flowers, fruit, wine, and incense to the spirits of the ancestors. Another popular ingredient of the sacrifice is the burning of special paper money, often called Hell Bank Money, which transfers its equivalent in cash to the spirits, giving them a more luxurious Afterlife. Such devotions are an act of veneration and respect to the spirits, and are also performed in the hope of their continued support with protecting the living family, and bringing good luck.

Food and drink that is not distributed among the graves is enjoyed as a picnic on the way home, giving rise to the notion that although the event may begin in a solemn mood, it ends in fun and happiness. The flying of kites is a particularly well-loved aspect of this festival, which looks to the future with optimism, while enjoying the present. This festival stands in contrast to the fearful Festival of Hungry Ghosts (see page 165).

Lady of the Dead, Mictecacihuatl. The Lady is still honored as a protector of the dead and statues of her abound in Día de los Muertos festivities. She is often associated with an owl, spider, or bat, which are her emblems. Her husband, the Lord of the Dead, is traditionally depicted as a blood-spattered skeleton.

Symbols of hope
In the myths of the Aztecs (also known as Mexicas), humanity was created from the bones of the gods who sacrificed themselves, and this sort of recycling of bones will be repeated in times to come. So human bones are not regarded as the fearful objects that many Western cultures hold them to be; instead they are a promise of new life to come. They are symbols of hope, and as precious as seeds.

Sugar skulls
It is no wonder, then, that sugar skulls are a favorite treat made especially for the festivities, to the delight of children and the souls of the dead alike. These and other playful effigies of a skeletal

nature are often placed on private altars in people's homes, or on tombs to nourish the souls.

Special trips

The bright orange flowers of the marigold are also favored ingredients in the festival, during which a special trip is usually made to the cemetery to clean and decorate the ancestral graves, and where the whole family shares a picnic while remembering and communing with the spirits of their dead.

RESPECTING THE DEAD

Tomb-sweeping Day is when Chinese people pay their respects to the dead. The most common customs include burning paper money that can be spent in the Afterlife, placing food, cigarettes, and decorations in the cemetery, and cleaning loved ones' gravestones.

The Science of Ghosts

The earliest science was carried out with no other instruments than the mind, and as technology developed scientists became used to redefining their ideas about the world. Science has often turned its attention to the paranormal, with mixed results, but recent developments in parapsychology are bearing important fruit. "Neurothology" was coined by Aldous Huxley in his 1962 novel *Island*, and although it is generally regarded as pseudoscience, the scientific investigation of religious and ghostly phenomena as an aspect of the brain's natural working is anything but fictitious. Millennia of dualism in Western culture, separating matter from spirit, body from soul, was softened in the closing decades of the 20th century by the mind-body-spirit movement. The intercession of mind to link the two extremes of body and soul has been an invaluable aid in integrating people under stress, alienated from the natural environment.

SPIRIT OF SCIENCE

In the 1980s, Dr. Michael A. Persinger popularized the idea that religious experiences could be produced by epileptic seizures of the temporal lobes. Many artists are supposed to have been inspired to divine communion by temporal lobe epilepsy, including the Russian novelist Fyodor Dostoevsky, who claimed to touch God during seizures. Mystics suspected of having this challenging medical condition include Joan of Arc, St. Paul, and Moses.

The "God Helmet"

The Canadian neuroscientist went on to devise a means of stimulating this effect artificially by creating low-intensity magnetic fields that emulate the brain's neural activity (a form of transcranial magnetic stimulation.) The device, which was worn on the subject's head, was soon dubbed the "God Helmet" because of the religious feelings it seemed to produce. Dr. Persinger's findings have not been accepted wholeheartedly into the mainstream of his profession because early attempts at replicating his results were not entirely successful, but the compelling anecdotal evidence he produced was quickly embraced by many enthusiasts of the paranormal.

Magnetic fields

Strong magnetic fields are known to affect brain function, and pulsed fields of one or two teslas are sometimes used to treat neurological illness such as depression, but Dr. Persinger experimented with fields as weak as one or ten microtesla— equivalent to those generated by common electrical equipment such as computer screens and hairdryers.

The God Helmet choreographed a complex pattern of these magnetic fields close to the skull, just above the ears. Although the subjects were alone in a sound- and light-proof room, 80 percent of them claimed to sense an eerie

The Limbic System — Psychic Antenna?

 The reason people find religious experiences so compelling may be found in the brain's limbic system. Parapsychologists have studied how people experience ghosts and why these experiences, like religious experiences, have such a profound effect on us. Located deep in the temporal lobe, the limbic system's job is to tag experiences with emotional importance. For example, the face of a close relative or friend is greeted with a warm emotional response, rather than the merely neutral recognition that, say, a co-worker might produce.

RELIGIOUS EXPERIENCE

The limbic system becomes highly active during a religious experience, instantly tagging every detail with enormous personal significance. If the limbic system becomes particularly active during a certain episode, that event may become the cornerstone of a lifetime's devotion, even becoming more important than the person's own life. Perhaps this is why people tend to treat sacred rituals as time-honored, never to be changed.

Sufferers from temporal lobe epilepsy often describe powerful religious experiences that take place during their seizures. On the other hand, Alzheimer's disease attacks the limbic system and sufferers not only lose their memory of loved ones, but also tend to lose their sense of the importance of religious beliefs. The big question is: does the brain create an illusion of religious experience as a side effect of the way it works, or is the limbic system stimulated by the immanence of divinity, making it into some sort of psychic antenna?

presence there with them. Depending on their personal beliefs, the subjects variously interpreted the presences as being God, Jesus, a deceased relative, or simply a certainty that they were not alone. Other apparently induced sensations included feeling weightless, or being pulled up out of the chair and floating around the room. Surges of powerful emotions, such as fear and anger, were also reported.

OUTSIDE THE LABORATORY

Experience-inducing fields are not commonly generated by domestic electrical equipment, and ordinary EMF meters (see page 125) are unsuited to the task of identifying them, making them difficult for the amateur paranormal investigator to spot. However, any sheet of a magnetic material, such as iron or steel, which is exposed to a magnetic field, will produce a distortion in

Muncaster Castle Hauntings

A set of magnetic fields remarkably similar to those generated by the God Helmet (see page 50) was discovered at one of Britain's most haunted ancient castles: Muncaster Castle, near the village of Ravenglass, Cumbria, is well known for its ghosts.

Guests sleeping in the Tapestry Room have often complained of disturbed nights and the feeling of a supernatural presence in the room with them. These are attributed to the ghostly antics of Tom Fool, a 16th-century jester. His pranks include door handles turning and doors opening when nobody is near. Inexplicable cold is also experienced and sometimes the sound of footsteps echo through the night, along with the cries and songs of disembodied voices.

Hazel Muir reported in the *New Scientist* magazine that Jason Braithwaite, a cognitive psychologist at the University of Birmingham, UK, tested the castle for magnetic anomalies. He found the Tapestry Room had the most complex magnetic fields and that these were associated with the bed, where an iron mesh supported the mattress.

Whenever a sleeper turned over, the bed generated magnetic fields immediately beneath the sleeper's pillow, fields whose strength and complexity were similar to those used by Dr. Persinger in the God Helmet.

that field when it vibrates. Such effects could be caused by sheets of corrugated iron flapping the wind, or steel filing cabinets in an office shaken by traffic on a busy road.

Fortunately, a combination of several factors is needed before problems may arise. The frequency of the magnetic field needs to be between once every ten seconds, and 30 times a second (0.1Hz and 30Hz). The strength or flux density of the field needs to be between 100 and 5,000 nanoteslas. And the field needs to vary in a complex way with variations of between one millisecond and two minutes.

Even given these particular conditions, our exposure needs to be for at least 20 minutes before effects are induced, and even then only about a quarter of the population seems susceptible. So if three or four people are in an identical EIF environment, only one might sense something that could be interpreted as a ghost.

THE QUEST FOR CONSCIOUSNESS
In recent decades scientists have been able to research the nature of the soul without losing their credibility. Their studies have focused on what it is we call our individuality, our sense of personal identity, our self-awareness: our

consciousness. Mediums would recognize this as the part of us that survives physical death.

Descartes, father of modern philosophy

French philosopher René Descartes (1596–1650) coined the quip *cogito ergo sum*—"I think, therefore I am." Hailed as the father of modern philosophy, Descartes defined thought as everything of which he was conscious. So, we may expand his expression to "I am conscious that I am, therefore I am," or perhaps simply abbreviate it to "I am." The cry "I am!" is the ultimate expression of identity—both personal and divine.

Descartes pointed to the pineal gland in the brain as the connection point between the spiritual mind, or soul, and the physical body. And it seems he wasn't too far wrong, as its neighboring thalamus is the subject of modern attention. This part of the brain collects nerve signals from all the senses (except olfactory) via the spinal cord, and relays these through nerve fibers that spread out in all directions to the cerebral cortex.

Random decisions

In comparison with the whole of our mind, our self-awareness really is like the tip of an iceberg. Professor John-Dylan Haynes, working in Berlin at the Bernstein Centre for Computational Neuroscience, has recently demonstrated that when we make a leisurely random decision, the actual decision is made several seconds before we become conscious of the choice. The person running the experiment could know what we'd choose, before we did.

Rather like the mysterious eye floating above the apparently Masonic unfinished pyramid on the US one-dollar bill, our consciousness is a small part of a deeply integrated whole. But we should not think of our body as made merely of inert and senseless clay; it is instead dynamic and vibrant, powerfully affecting the mind in a complex feedback loop. These two elements are simply parts of the same being—a human being—you, me, everyone.

Beliefs in the Afterlife

Few modern scientists concern themselves with such grand philosophical ideas, but many psychologists are keenly interested in one aspect of spirituality. Why do vast populations of humanity choose to believe in such similar gods, yet fight merciless wars to prove the details of their particular form of worship is superior to all others? Could such unspeakable atrocities continue if the faithful stopped believing their soul would enjoy the reward of eternity in paradise? Is belief in life after death fueling Hell on Earth?

2

Ghosts: Echoes in Time

Ghostly Repetitions

Some ghosts repeat the same actions every time they appear. It is as if they are part of a movie that keeps looping and replaying the same scene over and over again. Another way of looking at this is that an event has somehow imprinted itself onto its environment. Either way, witnessing such a haunting is watching history come to life.

UNCHANGING ECHOES

These echoes in time are unchanging and some seem to be fairly predictable, which means they are potentially verifiable. If such echoes could be proven, the discovery would change our understanding of the Universe, and would be a breakthrough of Nobel Prize proportions.

Because some of these echoes seem to manifest in a fairly predictable cycle—usually on an annual basis—it's only too tempting to lie in wait with an ambush of sensitive equipment in order to catch the next replay. And, because these ghosts do not seem to be living spirits, our investigation will not be hampered by an often-quoted theoretical prohibition on mankind finding proof of life after death.

Ghostly sounds

With sound, the biggest echoes follow the loudest bangs, so if there's one source of emotional output that could be expected to resonate powerfully through time it's the scene of a fiercely fought battle.

MARATHON BATTLE

The Greek traveler Pausanias recorded a ghost story he heard about Marathon, site of the famous battle in 490 BCE. Although his book, *Description of Greece*, was written several hundreds of years later, around the year 170 BCE, he says the haunting was still active.

Fighting ghosts

The plain where the battle had been fought was littered with the venerated tombs of fallen Athenian heroes, those who had paid with their lives to help secure victory over the Persian invaders. Every night their ghosts fought again and the sounds of their combat could be heard, mixed with the cries of their horses. Pausanias warned that to deliberately investigate this phenomena was looking for trouble. But people who wandered unawares into the midst of this supernatural mayhem would not find themselves endangered or caught up in it.

GHOSTS OF WAR

This illustration, from *Le Petit Journal*, Paris, 25 January 1903, shows Joseph Chamberlain (1836–1914) as Secretary of State for the Colonies, visiting South Africa, being confronted by the ghosts of the British troops killed during the second Boer War (1899–1902).

UK Wartime Ghosts

There have been some important battlefield hauntings over the centuries in the UK. Here is a small selection.

➤ *The sound of marching Roman feet was heard at Hardknott Fort, Cumbria, on 8 May 2007. The ghostly Legionaries were heard marching on a stone surface, though grass now covers the site.*

➤ *The Battle of Nechtansmere, near Dunnichen, Scotland, occurred in May 685 and resulted in a decisive Pictish victory against the Northumbrian king. On the night of 2 January 1950, a woman whose car had broken down found herself walking through the scene of the battle. For more than ten minutes she watched ghostly figures of men clad in leggings and brown tunics prowling the site by the light of flaming torches, searching among the bodies for friends and kinsmen.*

➤ *The island of Iona, Scotland, is famed as a Christian sanctuary. Its wealth attracted the attention of Viking raiders, whose ghostly longboats have been seen entering its harbor, with the marauders disembarking onto the island. Monks have also been seen and the sound of their chanting heard.*

➤ *On 4 October 1066, Harold was defeated in battle with the Normans at Battle, near Hastings. The Saxon king's bloodied ghost is said to haunt the battlefield. On the anniversary some say they have seen the arrow that fatally pierced his eye. A Norman knight on horseback is also said to ride across the battlefield on the same date.*

➤ *The opening battle in the Wars of the Roses was fought on 22 May 1455 and has left an imprint in the shopping center at the heart of St. Albans. Chequer Street still sometimes resounds to the noise of the hand-to-hand fighting.*

➤ *The ghosts of naked men are said to have been seen near the river at East Stoke, Nottinghamshire. Local tradition identifies them as Irish mercenaries who fought for the Earl of Lincoln in the Wars of the Roses. They had been defeated at the Battle of East Stoke in 1487 and had been stripped as a humiliation.*

➤ *The Battle of Sedgemoor, near Westonzoyland, Somerset, took place on 6 July 1685, and many events in this episode of the Monmouth Rebellion appear to have been imprinted on the landscape. As well as the sounds of battle that may be heard on the anniversary, there are many sites near by where people were hanged. One such site, Heddon Oak, had a hanging tree that fell long ago, but the stench of rotting flesh, the clanking of iron chains, and the groans of the dying rebels remain to this day.*

➤ *The Battle of Killiecrankie, Scotland, in which Highlanders of the Jacobite Rising defeated the troops of King William III, took place on 27 July 1689. The battle is replayed on its anniversary, including such details as the young women of the victorious side picking over the corpses of their slain enemies, collecting the spoils of war.*

The American Civil War

 The town of Gettysburg, Pennsylvania, is famous for the ferocity of the battle that raged there from 1–3 July 1863, and it is now claimed as one of the most haunted sites in the United States.

The many brutal sounds of warfare, including gunfire and screaming men, have been heard in the area, particularly around Devil's Den, which was the scene of wave after wave of fighting on 2 July as Confederates attacked and eventually took this stronghold from the Union. As well as the sounds of slaughter, a ghostly rider who vanishes inexplicably, has been seen here.

TAKING THE LIFT

The battleground shifted constantly and engulfed the town itself, including Pennsylvania College (now Gettysburg College), and here two college administrators found that the lift took them further than they dreamed possible. When the doors opened in the basement of Pennsylvania Hall, instead of storage space they saw a makeshift operating theatre, with patients lying all over the floor. They watched as doctors treated the wounded from the battle. At a time when amputation was the standard remedy for gunshot wounds and anesthesia

was unavailable, the sight was ghastly. Fortunately witnesses only saw the vision — there were no sounds. Eventually the lift responded to their repeated attempts to close the doors on this horrific scene and they were hoisted back into the present time.

During the battle, the stench of death in the town was said to be almost unbearable. After the Confederates had lost and withdrawn, and it was safe to walk the streets once more, the women used perfumes, such as peppermint and vanilla, to overcome the reek of blood. These sweetening scents are said to sometimes linger in the air to this day.

BLOODIEST DAY

The violent Battle of Antietam raged near Sharpsburg, Maryland, making the day of 17 September 1862 the bloodiest day of the Civil War. A sunken road held by Confederate forces was the scene of such carnage, as it was attacked and eventually overrun, that it became known by the name of Bloody Lane. The sounds and smells of gunfire and the ghosts of Confederate troops have been seen and heard there. At nearby Pry House, a Unionist headquarters, the ghost of a woman has been seen gazing out of an upstairs room, even though the room had no floor at the time.

IN TIMES OF PEACE

Not all imprinted hauntings (those that are recorded on the environment of the site, to be played back repeatedly) are violent in origin. And perhaps the reason the wartime cases have lasted so long is that the emotions were extreme and affected so many people, not least those who survived the fighting. But there are a great many other cases where the preserved events are of a peaceful nature. In some the emotion recorded is enjoyment, and in many experiences the presence is loving.

Admired mosaics

Early in the 1930s, the Swiss psychiatrist Carl Jung visited Ravenna, Italy. He and a friend paid a special visit to the Orthodox Baptistry and fell into a discussion about the mosaic frescoes that depicted scenes such as the Children of Israel crossing the Red Sea and the baptism of Jesus at the River Jordan.

There were four mosaics in all and Jung was deeply moved by them. They were not only beautiful in the wonderful, gentle, blue light, but the themes on the mosaic panels spoke to him of the mysteries of baptism. In particular, he was impressed by the depiction of Jesus walking on water and holding his hand out to Peter, who was afraid of sinking into the Sea of Galilee. Jung and his friend stood admiring and discussing this image for 20 minutes or more.

Photographic evidence

It wasn't until Jung tried to obtain photographs of the mosaics that he discovered they did not exist.

When he broke the news to his friend she refused to believe him at first, preferring to trust the evidence of her own eyes.

The duration of the incident, and the fact that the witnesses corroborated each other's testimony, make this an exceptional case. Given that the principal witness was a world-class psychiatrist, supremely well equipped intellectually to spot a trick of the mind, it is highly significant that Jung could not explain it away. In his autobiography, he declared that this event was among the most curious of his entire life.

Time-traveling fair

The standing stones of Avebury Stone Circle, Wiltshire, UK, date to around 3,000 BCE, and the importance of this megalithic complex is recognized in its designation as a World Heritage Site. It is perhaps surprising, then, to find its most famous haunting may be only as ancient as the mid-19th century CE.

Local author Edith Olivier was driving toward the village at dusk when she saw what appeared to be a fair in the middle of the stone circle. She could see the lights and could hear the music coming from the various booths and attractions, but as she drew up to the circle she found it was silent, dark, and empty. Only later did she learn that there had indeed been fairs held at the site, but that the last had been early in the latter half of the 19th century.

The Purring Ghost

It seems that minerals, such as stone, brick, and mortar, are not unique in having the property of soaking up recordings of events. Antiques are particularly susceptible, too.

A charming example of this occurred in the village of Alfriston, half a dozen miles northwest of Eastbourne, Sussex, UK. Mrs. Williams wished to be comfortable writing some works of fiction and invested in an old wooden desk from a local second-hand store. The desk gave the appearance of having been converted from a dressing table and was far from the quality she'd sought, but it was the right size and shape and had the advantage of being instantly available.

An 18th-century Russian woodcut of a cat.

AN INVISIBLE COMPANION

Having installed it at home, Mrs. Williams lost no time in getting down to work and found that her inspiration flowed well. She also found something else. As she sat working, she had a companion; an invisible, purring cat. At first she assumed it simply must have been a real cat sitting in the sunshine outside her window. But when she heard it while the rain was beating on the glass, she realized cats don't normally purr in the rain. It soon dawned on her that she only heard the creature when she was sitting at the desk and then she realized that the sound was coming from under the desk, as if the cat was curled up comfortably beside her feet.

She grew so accustomed to the animal's frequent companionship that she wasn't at all alarmed when it began brushing against her legs. Once, though, she did get a bit of a shock when the affectionate animal jumped lightly up onto her knees.

EXPLANATION

Not long after this episode, Mrs. Williams visited the second-hand store again and enquired after the provenance of the desk. The store keeper told her that it had previously belonged to an old woman who had owned and bred Siamese cats.

Whatever the explanation, as soon as she understood the origin and accepted the presence of the spirit cat, it ceased to manifest. Mrs. Williams never again heard or felt her furry, purring companion.

A Faithful Companion

The strength of the emotional bonds we can make with animals means that when a loved pet dies, the sense of bereavement really is like losing a member of the family. It is only natural that whenever we look at the place where their food used to be, we remember them there. When we walk past their favorite place to lie in the lounge, habit still guides our steps to walk around them. In grief we find them a constant companion, our memories of them are such that wherever we look, we see them there.

Those memory ghosts do fade because despite our feelings in those first sharp days of separation, time does heal. But these animal friends never leave us entirely—we will always cherish their lives. Even a hardened sceptic will understand this aspect of human nature. The following story is harder to explain.

THE DOG IN THE SHADOWS

Saturday 19 April 2008 was a memorable day for David Phillips. He had co-founded Torbay Investigators of the Paranormal (TIP) in 1995 and since then had sought evidence of paranormal activity, but he had never seen a ghost—until now. He was following up a lead and had arranged to call at the landowner's house. When he arrived he was asked to wait in the hall. From there he had a clear view into the lounge, where he saw what he assumed was a discarded sweater behind the sofa.

The rest of the house looked immaculate, so his attention returned to the out-of-place item. Then he saw it was a dog—gray and black—in the shadows. Then the owner arrived and the dog was forgotten until a lull in the

A tiled panel of a dog eating a bone (17th century, Portuguese.)

conversation, when David commented on the black Labrador lying in front of the fireplace, looked around and asked where the other dog had gone. The owner grew quiet. They had had another dog, he admitted, but it had died ten days ago. On the mantlepiece was a framed photograph of the black dog with its mother— a black and gray, Labrador–springer spaniel cross. This was a potentially awkward moment, but the owner admitted that one of the favorite places where the old dog would lie was right where David had seen it.

Search for an Explanation

What becomes of the present moment when it slips into the past is a great mystery. And what of the future—are we hurtling toward a fate that already exists and is predetermined, or is our destiny utterly formless and void until we create it? Time is a puzzle that ghosts may help to solve.

THE STONE TAPE

The best-known description of ghostly echoes in time is known as a "stone tape." It suggests that events can be recorded by the fabric of buildings. These impressions can be noticed by sensitive people who witness a replay of the event.

A moment of crisis

Anecdotal evidence suggests that many, if not most, ghosts of the recorded variety are enduring a moment of crisis, and strong emotions may be the key to understanding this sort of ghost. We know how powerful emotions can feel, and we don't need to be psychic to see when someone is in the grip of passion. Could these emotions somehow radiate out of us, to be soaked up by our surroundings?

Academics in the paranormal research community object to the word "theory" in connection with the stone-tape idea, because it doesn't actually propose a scientific experiment that could produce evidence in support of its hypothesis. Neither is there a clearly defined mechanism by which the event could become imprinted on the environment, nor is the method by which playback is set in motion adequately described. The phrase "stone tape" is generally accepted as having been coined by Nigel Kneale in his supernatural horror play *The Stone Tape* (1972). But the idea had been around for some time before that date: the controversial archeologist, paranormal researcher, and author Thomas Charles Lethbridge published the idea of hauntings involving a combination of a projector and a receiver in his book *Ghost and Ghoul* in 1961. Some attempts have been made to identify common features of repeated hauntings in the environment. The presence of water has been suggested as conducive to embedding the event, or quartz in the bedrock, but such studies are still far from complete.

Residual haunting

An alternative phrase to describe this type of haunting is "residual" haunting. This seems to imply that there is a residue left behind by the event. How this residue attaches itself to the haunted location is unclear, but it allows for psychics to come and cleanse the place of residual energy, removing traces of the haunting. This name has been rendered in German as *restligeist*—literally residual ghost. But there is a far more ancient precedent for the stone-tape idea—magic.

63

The Akashic Record

 Imagine a "book of life;" the present day may be a page somewhere in the middle. Our past is contained in the pages we have already read, and the pages we have yet to read continue our story into the future. Some people think the future pages are already written, while others believe they are blank until we write them. Either way, we are as free to act here and now as we can be.

Now imagine that there is a larger book, one that contains not only our own life, but everything that has ever existed, and everything that will exist. This book records all things from the beginning of time to the end of eternity. This vast repository has been called the Akashic Record (or Akashic Library), a name coined by Theosophists in the 19th century. On a personal level, the Akashic Record contains a record of all our actions, thoughts, and circumstances—all the information needed to judge a soul.

A SPIRITUAL LIBRARY

Some people say the Akashic Record is separate from physical reality, to be accessed like a "spiritual library," where advanced souls go to learn more about life and themselves. There, they may browse its contents at leisure, particularly if they are between incarnations, when they may select a time in which to be reborn, homing in to the precise child they wish to become. By doing this, they learn to see life from many points of view, gradually gaining a comprehensive view of life—omniscience.

THE UNIVERSE

Other people believe the Akashic Record is actually the Universe, which surrounds us and of which we are part—and that the past and future are completely formed, just out of reach of our senses. Our consciousness moves through this permanent body of events. We can only go in one direction—into the future. Some physicists share this view and regard time as an illusion created by the physiology of our consciousness in which the past, present, and future exist simultaneously in a unified continuum encompassing the entirety of space-time. This may sound exactly like the Akashic Record, but there is a key difference. Scientists do not consider there is any purpose to this Universe: there is no judgment of souls. We are independent of spiritual hierarchy, free to make our own judgments, according to our own conscience, changing our minds as we go along. But what of precognitive visions? Are they glimpses of the Akashic Record, gazing forward through the dimension of time?

Meeting Yourself Coming Back

A strange incident occurred to the 18th-century German author Johann Wolfgang von Goethe, who met himself while horse-riding toward Drusenheim, France. He clearly saw himself, in his mind's eye, riding toward him. His other self was wearing distinctive clothes he'd never seen before, gray in color, with gold.

A SENSE OF CALM
He had been upset at the time and found the vision a welcome distraction from his personal sadness. It had given him a sense of calmness and self-possession.

THE SAME CLOTHES
Eight years later, he found himself riding along that stretch again, wearing exactly the same clothes that he had seen himself wearing before—ones he had not chosen himself.

This may have been a premonition by glimpsing into the Akashic future (see opposite page), or perhaps it was it a greatly extended arrival apparition (see page 21).

Sapphire and Steel

 A variation on the stone-tape theme was used to great effect in the first season of the cult TV series *Sapphire and Steel* (1979) starring Joanna Lumley and David McCallum. The six episodes of *Escape Through a Crack in Time* portray how the ghosts, described as "visual refractions" of past events, could lie latent in old buildings and antique objects and be triggered into a replay by reciting old nursery rhymes. These harmless replays were interfered with and their energy subverted by entities that crossed through from beyond our time. The formerly inert haunting began producing poltergeist phenomena with life-threatening force. The task fell to Sapphire and Steel to neutralize this supernatural invasion. This was achieved by cornering it into a single object, freezing it to absolute zero (-273°C) and breaking it into myriad pieces. The team also dealt with ghosts in the Season Two (there were six in all), *The Railway Station*, where a human life was exchanged for innumerable souls that had been captured by a mysterious darkness. But those were sentient ghosts, not the stone-tape sort, so we must leave them, and move on.

THE STONE TAPE, THE PLAY

Aired on TV as a Christmas ghost story in 1972, this play by Nigel Kneale explored the idea that some events may be recorded in the fabric of buildings and when they are replayed, they appear as ghosts. The play was so successful that the name stuck as a description of residual hauntings.

SAPPHIRE AND STEEL

In *Escape Through a Crack in Time* (1979, written by P.J. Hammond) Sapphire and Steel (Joanna Lumley and David McCallum) combat invaders that harness the paranormal properties of household antiques and old nursery rhymes, such as those loved by the child Helen (Tamasin Bridge).

Talismans

 Shamans and other magicians have been energizing objects for millennia. By studying this tradition we may gain insights into how some ghosts are created and what triggers their manifestation. They use willpower to imbue the talisman with a meaning that can be remembered and released in some sort of manifestation. In the jargon of magic the raising of the energy is often called "conjuring a spirit," and this spirit is then directed to enter and reside in a material object—the talisman.

HOW TALISMANS WORK

Talismans, it is thought, work in the following way. When you are enjoying a summer holiday and your mood is light and free, you may find yourself gazing at an object that somehow captures every aspect of the way you are feeling—this could be a toy camel or a sea shell—and you instantly reach out for it and buy it, without thinking twice.

When you are back home and the winter rain is falling dismally, you may catch sight of that frivolous object and you'll experience your mood lifting. In that moment, your soul will feel joyful and the memories of who you met and where you went will replay brightly in your mind. Magic. A souvenir, such as a childhood toy, can do this effortlessly. Imagine how much more powerful an object could be when it is deliberately and repeatedly charged with a particular emotion. Magicians use all sorts of carefully researched choreography to build up their ceremony. Every aspect of the ritual is designed to focus attention on the emotion they seek to conjure. With every moment of concentration the energy gets stronger and this can build up for hours, or even days.

SYMBOLS AND RITUALS

We may view this sort of procedure with scepticism, but we are all familiar with, and actually use, much the same process in everyday life. The meticulous preparation for a wedding is a prime example, with its emphasis on symbolic color-coding and the ceremonial. This all culminates in the giving and receiving of rings—the tangible symbol of the love shared by the happy couple—often prized above all other possessions.

The attachment we have to items of sentimental value (a greatly underrated term) is the main reason why many household burglaries are so tragic. When we lose these treasured, magical, items we are not only poorer, but we feel violated. It is as if part of our very soul has been brutally amputated.

SHAMAN'S FLY WISK AND TALISMANS

Anything can be a talisman, but many are chosen because they have an inherent meaning—such as spiralling seashells (the winding path of life), feathers (associated with superhuman abilities such as flying), nuts (potential for new life), and bones (death and the Afterlife.) The ultimate talisman is our own body.

PSYCHOMETRY

Ceremonial objects with symbolic value, such as wedding rings and medals, may seem far removed from souvenirs such as beach pebbles and knick-knacks, but they can all trigger powerful psychological processes. They can influence our moods (whether consciously or unconsciously) and may even recall memories that are as vivid as any ordinary experience.

Spirit battery

But are these keepsakes a sort of spirit battery that can be charged with psychic energy, ready to release it on cue? If so, then someone else should be able to have the same reaction as we do. If a treasure is stolen and sold, the new owner should be able to sense the same emotions and share the same memories that it inspired in us. Many people believe this to be true. It is not unusual, for instance, for somebody browsing in an antiques store to spot something that fires their imagination. They can tell at a glance, or at first touch, that the item has been loved, that it was cherished by an elderly lady who had owned it since she was a child, that she often admired it beside an open window overlooking a sunny rural garden... or that it was an ignored beacon of hope consigned to a dark corner of a home riven by discord and domestic violence...

PSYCHOMETRY IN ACTION

This photograph, taken during the 1920s by Harry Price, shows a medium holding a personal item against her forehead, in this case a glove, in the hope of sensing information about its owner.

Such impressions are surprisingly common examples of involuntary psychometry—the reading of an object to divine its history. Pre-owned clothes and jewelry, in particular, seem to convey the character of the person who wore them, and such purely subjective impressions can make or break the sale. While it is rarely possible to check the accuracy of such impressions in a shop, you can set up a variety of experiments to investigate this element of clairvoyance or ESP (extra-sensory perception). Because the standard of scientific proof is so high, it is notoriously

A Home Experiment in Psychometry

 Everyone brings a small item from home; something they have owned for years. One by one, the owners put them into a bag, taking care no one sees. The items are jumbled up and then everyone takes one out. Handling the object for a few minutes, in silence, everyone tries to build up a picture of the surroundings in which the object has been. Perhaps ideas will come of events that have taken place in its presence.

Some people hold the objects to their forehead and imagine it projecting pictures into their mind. Others project themselves inside the object, imagine it is back where it belongs, and then open their spiritual eyes. It is fine to use logic and deductive reasoning, along with physical senses.

Each person talks about what they feel about the object they are holding and the actual owner verifies every detail. It is best to leave the owner's remarks until all the readings have been given (otherwise the last person reading will know by process of elimination who owns the object they are holding.) At the end, the group discusses techniques people used and ideas for making the experiment better. The key to success seems to be to repeat the process over several sessions, allowing everyone to get used to the way it feels when their choice is right and wrong.

difficult to conduct convincing experiments, even in a laboratory. However, as long as you accept the fact that results of your investigation may be flawed (it is particularly difficult to screen out telepathy, for instance), you may gain a good deal of practical experience.

PSYCHOMETRY AND GHOSTS
Even if you find your readings are not as accurate as you might hope, you should discover much about the way your mind operates when confronted with puzzles that cannot be solved using the physical senses. Pay special attention to the changes you feel when you start to open up to an object. And you should learn how to withdraw from that object and break away from it.

What you have learned in the comfort of your own home can be put to practical use at the site of a haunting simply by reaching out a hand and touching a wall. Of course, the power stored in a haunted house is much stronger than that in a thimble from a friend's sewing box. You should approach such a site with a good deal of caution and not allow yourself to open up hastily. It is important to feel in control of what you are doing

Psychic Quests

 The 1988 movie *Vibes*, pairs museum psychometrist Nick Deezy (Jeff Goldblum) with spirit medium Sylvia Pickel (Cyndi Lauper) to produce a memorable comedy in which they are duped into hunting for Inca gold by amiable con man Harry Buscafusco (Peter Falk).

Nick and Sylvia first meet at an ESP (extra-sensory perception) testing laboratory, where he uses his gift to describe the history of a variety of objects and she communicates with her spirit guide. At first Nick doesn't want to go on Harry's quest, but when he discovers that his fiancée has been unfaithful he finds himself at a loose end and the unlikely team join forces, following clues only they could find.

INSIGHTS INTO THE SPIRIT WORLD

The unraveling of mysterious clues, each leading to another, is a feature of a psychic quest, in which people try to achieve insights into the spirit world or find amulets of power. These quests may begin anywhere and with any or no purpose in mind. By some method, ranging from mediumship or psychometry to divination, or even dreams, a second location is identified. When the team arrives there, they once again set about seeking whatever they can find.

SIGNIFICANT PLACES

In the case of a haunting, the quest might identify a succession of significant places where the spirit manifests, to build up a picture of their life and message. So although they may manifest strongly where they died, further manifestations may be located at different places. For example, the ghost of Anne Boleyn, the first of Henry VIII's wives to be executed, is said to haunt Blickling Hall, Bollin Hall, Hampton Court Palace, Hever Castle, Lambeth Palace, Marwell Hall, Rochford Hall, Salle Church, and the Tower of London.

Similarly, the ghost of President Abraham Lincoln, who himself attended seances, haunts not only the White House and Ford's Theatre in Washington, but is also seen in Springfield, Illinois, at his tomb at Oakridge Cemetery, in the vicinity of the original courthouse, and at his former home. He has also been seen at Fort Monroe, Virginia.

Just as a movie takes us from scene to scene as the story unfolds, so the psychic quester travels from place to place, collecting piece after piece of the jigsaw. Following these clues may take a good deal of time, but some believe it to be one of the most rewarding of all paranormal pastimes.

at such a site, and as soon as you feel you might be losing your sense of security, back away and close your mind to it. If you have any difficulty in severing the link, so that you cannot stop the resonance in your mind, your companions should rally around to help. If necessary, they should bring the investigation to an immediate halt and take you to a place of safety.

Stored memories

The possibility of sensing the stored memories of a haunted house is a powerful attraction to many people, and even those who have no desire to speak with the spirits of the dead may enjoy this pursuit just out of interest. Seeing these stone-tape projections of the past may be the closest

VIBES

Hired to find a missing person, Nick Deezy (Jeff Goldblum) uses psychometry, while Sylvia Pickel (Cyndi Lauper) consults her spirit guide in the movie adventure *Vibes* (1988). Their journey leads them to a lost Inca city, where they contact forces beyond their ability to control.

you ever come to so-called time travel, and there is already a healthy market in such supernatural tourism. Sadly, though, very few of these tourists have trained themselves properly to appreciate the places they visit.

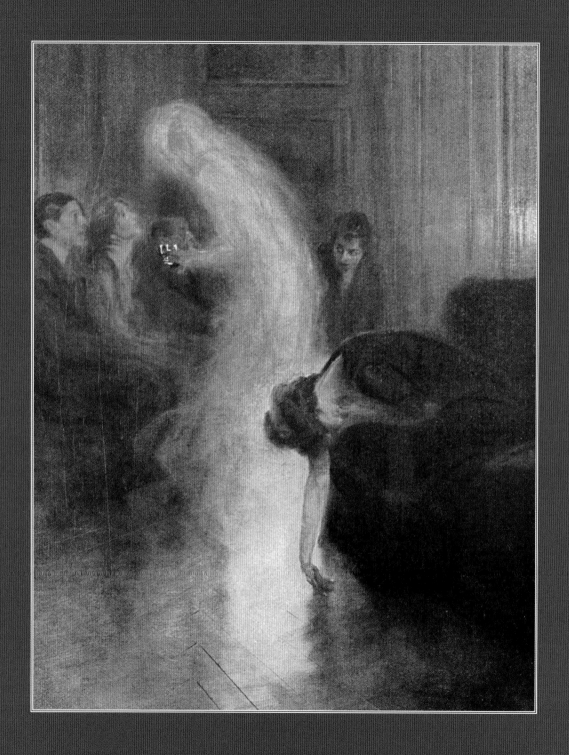

3

Interactive
Ghosts

Parapsychology

Parapsychology studies psychological phenomena that are beyond the scope of science to explain. Its three main areas are known as telepathy, psychokinesis, and clairvoyance, all of which can be demonstrated by mediums and poltergeists. Not all parapsychologists accept that these phenomena are caused by spirits of the dead, preferring to suppose the powers of the living are sufficient to explain them. Some people believe there is a spiritual law that prohibits hard evidence of the soul's survival after bodily death. For these believers, faith is the vital key that opens the door to the spiritual realm and once inside they find all the evidence they need.

Of course, science doesn't work that way, so for a long time these two groups of people—the research scientists and the practicing mediums—were barely on speaking terms. However, the new academic discipline of parapsychology is bridging that divide by studying the psychology of paranormal experiences.

COMMUNICATING GHOSTS

One of the biggest debates is over the existence of ghosts that actively communicate with people. This controversy has been raging fiercely since time immemorial, but was raised to a new pitch in the 19th century, when the public imagination was captured by the activities of the Fox sisters, who became interested in communicating with the spirit world (see box opposite.)

Mediumship

However, the tradition of public demonstrations of mediumship continues to this day. The British census of 2001 ranked spiritualism as the eighth-largest faith group in the nation, with 32,000 people claiming allegiance and spiritualist churches everywhere continuing their mission to demonstrate proof of survival.

Most mediums deliver their messages free of charge, but there are still professionals willing to stand up in front of a paying audience and give them their money's worth by communicating messages from their departed loved ones.

TV mediums

American medium John Edward is a TV personality well known for his shows *Crossing Over with John Edward* (1999–2004) and *John Edward Cross Country* (2006–2008), which feature him delivering messages to an appreciative audience. Many of the people he addresses clearly believe his contact with their departed loved ones is genuine and the advice he gives them is helpful.

6ixth Sense

The same could be said of any number of performance mediums. The popular TV show *6ixth Sense* with Colin Fry (2002), showcases the talents of a man who is today widely regarded as among the most successful spiritualist

The Beginnings of Spiritualism

If a religion can be said to have begun with a single incident, perhaps spiritualism's moment came on the night of 31 March 1848, when the Fox family lived in Hydesville, near Arcadia, New York, in a house haunted by rapping sounds and other strange noises.

On that fateful evening the youngest daughter, Kate, invited the spirit to follow her example and clapped her hands. The spirit obliged with corresponding raps, and so began a series of communications that eventually codified into a system using one knock for "yes," and two knocks for "no."

Margery Crandon producing ectoplasm from her right ear.

Her sister Margaret also developed the ability to communicate with the spirit, and eventually it was divined to be a murdered peddler called Charles B. Rosma, who had been secretly buried in the cellar. Some human remains were recovered when the family excavated the site. Word of the sisters' abilities spread and soon the girls were traveling to give private seances and public demonstrations in both America and Europe. What marked them apart from other mediums was the physical nature of the replies from the spirit world. They started a trend that particularly captured the imagination of the upper and middle classes and numerous other mediums were soon following suit. Demonstrations included table-tapping, where a table would partially or fully levitate and knock responses on the floor.

Some mediums would place objects, such as trinkets or musical instruments, around the room and these would float around or make sounds by themselves. But perhaps the most famous of all physical manifestations was ectoplasm (see picture left), which was sometimes seen to flow from the mouth or ear of the medium as a gauzy white film. This might sometimes form into the features of the communicating spirit.

mediums in the UK. Billed for legal reasons as entertainment, the program focuses on Colin Fry presenting messages that come from the spirit world to the studio audience. Many of these messages seek to heal the emotional wounds that have been left by bereavement, while others attempt to solve a range of problems with words of wisdom drawn from the perspective of the spiritual world. Inevitably, these shows have their critics and detractors.

Detecting Fraud

 Almost all seances in the late 19th and early 20th centuries were conducted in very low light, or even in complete darkness. The potential for deception was enormous and, in time, many mediums were proved to employ tricks. One of the most vigorous and successful in the fight to expose fraudulent mediums was the stage magician Harry Houdini (see picture right). Ironically since he didn't believe in spiritualism, his ghost has allegedly been seen at his former home in California.

Many scientific thinkers also applied themselves to discovering the truth, establishing respected organizations such as the Society for Psychical Research in 1882. Some mediums, such as the Edinburgh-born Daniel Douglas Home, who was famous for levitating, were never caught cheating. But the publicity given to exposed hoaxers inevitably eroded public confidence.

In 1888 medium Margaret Fox (see page 77) confessed that she had made rapping noises during a session by loudly cracking her toe joints. Even though she later retracted her admission, it fueled controversy that saw the whole profession sliding into disrepute. Nearly a decade after her death, the chance discovery, in 1904, of a human skeleton at her house rekindled faith, for a while. But by the end of the 1920s, spiritualism had lost many of its wealthy and prestigious patrons.

THE SCEPTICS

Among the most outspoken critics against performance mediums are the professional sceptics, such as James Randi, and organizations such as the Committee for Skeptical Inquiry. They are relentless in their efforts to expose the techniques that fraudulent mediums use to trick and bamboozle their victims. Among the criticisms is the accusation that TV programs may be selective in what they show, by featuring successful communications while ignoring all the failed attempts.

HARRY HOUDINI'S SEANCE FRAUD

This photograph, taken in 1925, shows Houdini demonstrating how "ectoplasm" may be produced from the mouth and then wrapped convincingly around a mask. "Ectoplasm" was extremely easy to fake and seemingly "disappeared" when it came into contact with daylight.

Fishing exercises

Other criticisms are less charitable and suggest that mediums may mount fishing exercises by asking initially vague questions such as: "Does anyone recognize the name George?" This is known as the "cold reading technique," in which the medium homes in on whoever recognizes the name, making judgments about age, gender, and social group, to construct detailed questions and statements that lead to the person admitting to something dramatic.

The "hot reading technique" is far more controversial and involves researching the audience before the demonstration actually begins. This may be achieved by advisers collecting information before the show, or using hidden microphones to catch casual conversations among the audience during the wait before the medium takes the stage. A stooge may also be placed among the audience to get things going, particularly if the medium hits a dry patch in which few messages find anyone to accept them. Seeing somebody in the crowd breaking down in tears at an apparently correct message can help an audience relax and encourage them to behave similarly.

DEVELOPING MEDIUMSHIP ABILITIES

Different issues affect non-professional mediums; people just beginning to experiment with developing mediumistic abilities. These abilities can be mystifying. For example, if we are in a haunted building and an odd thought arises spontaneously, for example we suddenly see (with our mind's eye) happy children running

The dividing line between the world of the living and the realm of the dead is often described as being as insubstantial as a veil. Trying to separate the imaginary voices that naturally populate our thoughts, and the supposedly true voices of spirits that speak in our minds, can be as frustrating as trying to out-stare our own reflection.

up and down the stairs, is that imagination or clairvoyance? And if one of those children briefly smiles up at us and says "My name is Jane," is that imagination or mediumship? Most paranormal investigation groups allow people free rein to try to develop mediumship, encouraging them to simply say what they sense. These reports are recorded so that the group may research the site history to check those intuitive messages for accuracy.

Our caution regarding "cold reading techniques" applies in this case also—even if we uncover historical evidence of a person with the name communicated in the vigil, we must be wary of accepting commonly used names, such as Elizabeth or William, as evidence of contact with the spirit world. Further verifiable details should always be sought.

Ghost Whisperer, the TV Series

 Not all mediums are performers; most try to keep their gifts to themselves and only reveal them to others when absolutely necessary. This is the premise of the hit TV series *Ghost Whisperer*.

The title comes from the tradition of horse whispering, documented since the early 19th century, when Daniel Sullivan used unorthodox techniques to retrain traumatized horses. His process relied on developing trust between the animal and himself and involved close contact.

A similar approach is featured in this series, which focuses on ghosts who are unable to cross into the light. *Ghost Whisperer* first aired in 2005 and the pilot's opening scene shows a young girl at a funeral, approached by the ghost of the old man in the coffin, who asks her to give his wife a message of his undying love. The child asks for proof and the ghost describes the couple's intimate champagne toast to the moon and stars. The widow is comforted and the ghost is at peace, but the girl tells her grandmother that she doesn't understand—her grandmother assures her calmly that one day, she will.

The scene cuts to when the girl has grown to a young woman, the ghost whisperer Melinda Gordon (played by Jennifer Love Hewitt). The programs chronicle her efforts to help Earthbound spirits to cross over into the light. This is usually achieved either by bringing about a reconciliation between the deceased and the people left behind, or by Melinda doing something that was left undone, allowing the spirit to rest in peace.

Jennifer Love Hewitt, appearing in Ghost Whisperer, *"Leap of Faith" (Season Four, aired 13 March 2009.)*

Top Ten Mediums

This is a list of the top ten most well-known mediums worldwide:

➴ **Derek Acorah** Like many spirit mediums, Derek (born 1950, Liverpool, UK) was visited by the ghost of a close relative when he was a child. Best known for his work with the TV show Most Haunted, he has also written eight books. His spirit guide, Sam, was a friend from a previous incarnation 2,000 years ago, in what is now Ethiopia.

➴ **Allison DuBois** Psychic medium Allison (born 1972, Arizona, USA) is best known for the TV series Medium, which, while fictional, is inspired by her talents and experiences. She tours and has written several books.

➴ **John Edward** Psychic medium John (born 1969, New York, USA) is best known for TV shows Crossing Over with John Edward, and John Edward Cross Country, in which he offers the audience messages from loved ones who have passed over.

➴ **Witch of Endor** The medium, or as many translations of the Bible suppose, Witch of Endor (situated in modern Israel), is probably the most widely known and one of the bravest of all mediums. She was famously consulted by King Saul in 1007 BCE despite her services carrying a penalty of capital punishment.

➴ **Kate and Margaret Fox** Assured of their place in history as founders of modern spiritualism, Kate and Margaret (1837–1892, born in Consecon,

Canada; and 1833–1893, Bath, Canada, respectively) were international celebrity mediums, yet both died in poverty.

➴ **Colin Fry** Best known for his TV series 6ixth Sense with Colin Fry, this psychic medium (born 1962, Haywards Heath, UK) started training to be a professional medium aged just 17. He has been hailed as Britain's most popular medium.

➴ **John Holland** Psychic medium John (born 1961, Dorchester, USA) is a popular author with a particular interest in Tarot cards, having developed his own Psychic Tarot Oracle Cards. His books, including Spirit Whisperer, and his website detail his abilities and experiences.

➴ **Sally Morgan** Having seen her first ghost at the age of four, Sally (born 1951, London, UK) has been hailed as Britain's best-loved psychic. She is probably best known for her TV show Sally Morgan: Star Psychic, and has published books including an autobiography, My Psychic Life.

➴ **Doris Stokes** Having been visited by ghosts since her early childhood, Doris (1920–1987, born in Grantham, UK) achieved international celebrity as a medium in the 1970s. Her first book Voices in My Ear was published in 1981.

➴ **David Wells** Medium, astrologer, and Qabalist, David (born 1960, Kelloholm, UK) is best known for his stint with TV show Most Haunted, although his interests embrace a wide range of spiritual traditions and values. His website details his work with past lives.

COLIN FRY IN 6IXTH SENSE

Renowned for his caring approach, Colin brings great sensitivity and humor to his shows, in which he attempts to help members of the studio audience to communicate with friends and relatives who have passed to the other side.

Contact or Coincidence?

 The plight of those who died in battle is an enduring theme in ghost lore and many people are working to help alleviate the suffering of both spirits and bereaved.

In the build-up to D-Day (6 June 1944), a large part of the South Hams of Devon, UK, was commandeered by the military as a training ground for the Allied invasion of occupied France. Around 1.30 a.m. on the morning of Friday 28 April, nine German torpedo boats attacked a convoy heading for the training beach at Slapton Sands. Seven hundred and forty-nine US soldiers and sailors were killed or reported as missing in action. Many ghosts of the soldiers have been seen in the vicinity and the sounds of explosions out to sea have been heard on the anniversary of the convoy's destruction. A persistent rumor in the area insists that many of the bodies of the drowned were buried locally and mediums still try to find these sites in order to give the spirits rest.

One of these, Christine Donnelly, took part in a vigil as a psychic medium at Slapton Sands on Monday 28 April 2008. Just after 2 a.m. she became aware of "a man who was on board a ship and was in a room with lots of shelves, which were stacked with blankets, boxes, metal cups and plates, and dried foods, in fact all sorts of items stacked everywhere." He was Stevie Stephenson, from Illinois, USA. Christine "saw" a heavy metal door swing back and trap him behind it. "He was unable to push it back open again as it was being held in place by the weight of rushing water," she said.

Research later found a man with the surname Stephenson listed as missing in action on the 28th. He was member of the 3206th Quartermaster Service Company, which suffered many casualties that night and could account for the ghost's association with stored supplies. However, the dead man's name was James, not Stevie, and published official records variously say he enlisted either in Missouri or Maryland. However, Stevie is a standard nickname derived from the surname Stephenson.

Christine also saw the spirits of a group of men: "One of them held a large book, which had a rigid cover and a heavy metal spine. He held this book out to me and I was given this message: 'Remember us, don't forget us'." This book contained the names of those who lost their lives there but were still unaccounted for.

She was upset by the vivid impressions and messages that she received about the way the people died and their undying desire for repatriation. With the weight of US officialdom denying that there were any bodies left buried in the South Hams, the task of trying to find them was daunting, to say the least.

HAUNTED BY COINCIDENCE

Christine was in a quandary. Had she been chosen by the ghosts to finally solve the mystery? But her initial contacts with the spirits hadn't contained clear enough evidence to start digging anywhere, so could she afford to devote time to what might turn out to be an insubstantial quest? As she struggled to decide what to do, she seemed plagued by reminders of the crucial choice she had to make. Just two days after the vigil, Wednesday 30 April 2008, Christine, who worked as a nurse, was talking with an elderly patient when he told her he had actually been involved in the exercises at Slapton in World War II. Christine decided to start keeping a diary.

CHRISTINE'S DIARY

Tuesday 6 May 2008

"I had a look in the book-box, where patients leave books for others to read. There was nothing that interested me. A few minutes later I passed the book-box again. At the back was a large book entitled *D-Day: The Dramatic Story of the World's Greatest Invasion* by Dan Parry."

Tuesday 5 August 2008

"I'd been trying to get into a local church for the best part of a year. Today I was lucky and it was unlocked. A display on a table top was dedicated to 'All the American Servicemen who lost their lives in the D-Day rehearsals, some of whom had been stationed at nearby villages'."

Wednesday 3 September 2008

"Today I went to a supermarket. Two people were talking. As I walked away the man said suddenly in a very loud voice 'If you go back about 50 years to the D-Day landings...' I stopped in my tracks and thought 'Here we go again!' When I got home I picked up the local newspaper to see what had been happening in the area and after turning the page I read the Headlines 'Emotional trip back'."

Saturday 13 September 2008

"While walking along a lane in Blackawton with a local resident, she suddenly stopped and pointed to a field and said 'Apparently there are American soldiers buried here who were involved in the Slapton incident'."

Friday 11 December 2009

"I was returning home from Belfast and was at the airport. I went over to have a look at the bookshop. The first book that caught my attention was D-Day: The Battle for Normandy by Antony Beevor. I smiled to myself and thought 'No, surely it's not starting again.' After arriving home I checked my emails and found one from a local investigator. I phoned him and he started to talk about synchronicities and Slapton. So there it was again, after nearly a year of silence, twice in one day—the Slapton incident. Was the wheel of synchronicity about to turn full circle?"

Psychic Investigators

An area in which psychics are keen to offer their services is police investigations.

MURDER INVESTIGATION

A news story in 2009 revealed that police in Dyfed-Powys, Wales, had investigated reports from a medium that a man had been murdered. When the man, Carlos Assaf, had been found dead, his family had consulted with mediums and been told that he had died after being forced to drink bleach and petrol by gangsters. The police felt that their obligation to investigate all deaths thoroughly included a duty to reassure the family that all leads had been checked. The post mortem, however, showed that Mr. Assaf had died by hanging. The inquest heard that the deceased had had a row with his girlfriend and his death was recorded by the coroner as suicide.

Mistaken claims

Well-intentioned but mistaken claims can cost the police dearly. An estimated £20,000 was spent following up the false leads in the case of Mr. Assaf. In the first month after four-year-old Madeleine McCann went missing in 2007, police received reports from hundreds of psychics, each of which had to be investigated. Dr. Ciarán O'Keeffe of Derby University has made a study of psychics involved in police work and in ten years of research he has so far failed to find convincing evidence that psychic detectives have contributed accurate information. Dr. O'Keeffe is well known as the parapsychologist who provides the voice of reason in the popular TV show *Most Haunted*. His opinion on the value of psychic informers in police business, though, will disappoint many, because this should be one of the easiest ways to prove that mediumship works. In a murder case, for example, the ghost of the victim could be expected to have a strong desire for justice from the world of the living, possibly involving vengeance. The spirit might also wish to communicate with loved ones. Perhaps their unforeseen death has left undone something that still seems vitally important. These are all classic compulsions for ghosts to remain Earthbound. Any or all could apply to a murder victim.

Recovering remains

The theoretical links between body and spirit mean that in cases where the victim's body has not been found by conventional means, the ghost could ably assist the police in recovering mortal remains. With these ingredients in the mix, criminology seems the perfect arena for proof of the spirit's survival to be made public. It is sobering that Dr. O'Keeffe has publicly urged mediums to stop wasting police resources.

GHOST CRIME-BUSTERS

The idea of psychics leading the way to solving serious crimes, such as murder, was championed by Nordisk Film who made a reality TV series in which clairvoyants were introduced to real

From Murder to Missing Persons

Psychic medium Joe Power has risen to prominence in the field of psychic investigation, and says he has assisted the Metropolitan police, London, UK, with their enquiries by passing on messages from the victim in a murder investigation.

In his book *The Man Who Sees Dead People*, Joe reveals he started seeing ghosts at the age of three, and when he was five the spirit of his late Uncle Tom introduced himself by reassuring the lad that his father would survive a hospital visit. Tom was right about that and has been Joe's spirit guide ever since. Joe was overwhelmed by the numbers of dead people that visited him while he was young, at school, even at home when he tried to sleep at night. He likened his experience to that of Cole Sear in the movie *Sixth Sense*, but he sank into a vicious spiral of alcohol, gangs, and crime.

PSYCHIC ABILITIES
The death of his brother jolted Joe into a new lifestyle and he spent ten years researching mediumship to help him understand and deal with his paranormal experiences. Now in his mid-forties, Joe uses his psychic abilities in popular demonstrations of clairvoyance, seeking to prove to people that death is not the end. In 2009, *Soul & Spirit* magazine readers voted him the UK's Favourite Male Psychic. Joe's particular interest lies in helping solve crimes. His career as a psychic detective really began in 1999, when he dreamed of a woman with long, dark hair. She urged him to find her killer and her body. A series of visions ensued, and he realized he was communicating with the spirit of Lynsey Quy.

The 21-year-old woman had gone missing from her home in Southport, Merseyside, UK, in December 1998 and Power told police she had been killed by her husband. He also gave them information about the whereabouts of her body, saying it had been dismembered, with some parts buried at a fairground and others near a railway line. Although police failed to act on his insights, in June 2000 her torso was found near a roller-coaster and her arms and legs in bushes beside a railway. Her husband pleaded guilty to murder and was imprisoned for life. Joe also participated in the investigation to find Shannon Matthews, a schoolgirl who went missing from her home in Dewsbury, West Yorkshire, UK, for 24 days in 2008. During her ordeal, Joe was invited by the *People* newspaper to use his abilities to try to help solve the mystery of her disappearance.

They visited her home and met Shannon's mother, Karen, and her mother's partner Craig Meehan. Joe told them her abductor was associated with Craig and that his name was Michael or Mick. At this point, Craig left the room. Joe also sensed a connection with Batley and the name "Paul." When he mentioned this, Karen left the room. Within a week, police found Shannon in Batley Carr, at the home of Michael Donovan. He was Craig's uncle, known to use the alias Paul Drake. He received an eight-year sentence for kidnapping, false imprisonment, and perverting the course of justice. Despite these successes, Joe has admitted that it may take 30 to 40 years before we can expect mediums to make the breakthrough and start finding bodies.

NOT A HAPPY MEDIUM

In her emotionally tense investigation, Allison (played by Patricia Arquette) displays a picture which could help solve a man's murder in *Once in a Lifetime* (Season Six, Episode Eight.)

"cold case" crime situations. The show was so successful that in 2002 they started selling the rights to *Sensing Murder* in many countries including the USA, New Zealand, and Australia. The format of each episode is generally the same and begins by showing the viewer the known facts of the case. Then the audience is shown what the psychics and mediums said when they were first given an artefact from the crime scene or shown a photograph of the victim. This enables them to use psychometry to read the history of the crime. The clairvoyants are then taken to the crime scene and allowed to follow their intuition to locate new evidence which the police then evaluate. The show employs psychic mediums such as Kelvin Cruickshank and Sue Nicholson from New Zealand, and Deb Webber from Australia; while the US series opened with Pam Coronado and Laurie Campbell.

Impressive insights

When the show first aired it made compulsive viewing and the quality of the clairvoyants' insights seemed impressive. In New Zealand and Australia *Sensing Murder* has run to four seasons, with its American counterpart *Sensing Murder US* also proving popular. Sadly, though, despite tackling dozens of cases of murder and missing persons where the police investigations have stalled through lack of evidence, none of the leads offered by the psychics have yet successfully closed a single case. But then any new lead in a cold case is difficult to verify because so much time has elapsed, erasing both people's memories and the forensic evidence. In time it may yet be found that a clue revealed through exploring the paranormal means may achieve a conviction.

Investigators in TV Fiction

 Of course, in fiction, success in investigating the paranormal comes more easily.

RANDALL AND HOPKIRK (DECEASED)

The TV series *Randall and Hopkirk (Deceased)*, first aired in 1969, was a great hit. Set in London in the "swinging sixties," the 26-episode show followed the adventures of two private investigators, one of whom was dead and could find clues other detectives couldn't possibly find. The concept was remade in 2000 and aired for two seasons.

MEDIUM, THE TV SERIES

The popular TV series *Medium* stars Patricia Arquette in the role of real-life psychic medium Allison DuBois. It quickly gathered a fan base of eager viewers and has aired more than a hundred episodes. Set in Phoenix, Arizona, the first episode vividly establishes the characters. When Allison flies to Texas to help the Texas Rangers in their search for a six-year-old child, the sceptical captain tests her by visiting false locations. Allison senses the correct one even before they drive up to it. Here she meets the ghost of a girl—the victim's sister, who witnessed the attack. Outside the house Allison is drawn to a spot where she claims the boy is buried. The exhumation of the child's body is postponed because of the arrival of Hurricane Allison (2001), which destroys the evidence. However, in an interview with the suspect, she tells him he hadn't walked into the room alone—he was accompanied by the spirit of the man who molested him when he was a child. And that pedophile was followed by the man who assaulted him... and so on. Allison explains this is the chance to break the chain of evil and she wins a confession from him. Back in Arizona, she is hired as a consultant to the District Attorney's Office. Her first case is to interview a man whose wife had been found dead. It is the interview she has dreamed of at the beginning. Unfortunately, official corroboration of her involvement with the Texas Rangers appears to have been conspicuous by its absence.

That the series has already run to six seasons is proof of the deep appeal of the show's premise that wrongs can be righted, that one woman can make a difference, and that the dead can attain justice and finally be laid to rest. Audiences appear to derive a great sense of satisfaction when they see their champion facing terrible ordeals, including battling nightmarish psychic threats, to ensure wrongdoers don't literally get away with murder.

Ghost, the Movie

The movie *Ghost* (1990) is a romantic comedy that can generate tears of heartache and mirth in equal measure. This sort of evidence depicted in the movie is often claimed as the most compelling demonstration of survival of the spirit and is frequently used during stage performances by professional mediums. But sceptics who have researched such claims of intimate knowledge have found the evidence flawed. This is because the bereaved are so keen to believe that they are wiling to accept even vague statements as proof. Our desire to hear a message of comfort from a loved one can easily overpower our discernment.

AN INVISIBLE GHOST

Ghost is set in middle-class New York, where ceramic artist Molly Jensen (Demi Moore) and banker Sam Wheat (Patrick Swayze) are setting up home. Walking home one night, Sam is killed in a mugging. A gentle light streams down, entrancing Sam's soul, but when Molly cries out in grief, he instinctively goes to her side. The light departs, leaving Sam as an invisible ghost watching over his grieving fiancée, unable to contact her. Sam discovers that Molly is still in danger from the mugger and when he sees a medium's parlor he enters. The medium, Oda Mae Brown (Whoopi Goldberg), is a phoney, but she

hears Sam. He persuades her to warn Molly. Sam uses intimate language that only she would know, convincing her that Oda Mae is telling the truth.

DUEL BETWEEN GOOD AND EVIL

In *Ghost* the story continues with an intricately woven yet well-paced series of comedic and romantic scenes. And Sam develops the power to move objects by directing his emotions into the pit of his stomach and then letting them explode into physical action. Eventually Sam confronts the man responsible for his death. In this duel between good and evil, played out between the living and the dead, the enemy is killed. But no white light streams down to collect his soul. Instead, the shadows start to move. They flow toward his ghost, taking the forms of terrifying humanoid spirits. Clutching him in a smothering embrace, they drag him away screaming into the distance.

Now Molly is safe and the white light reappears for Sam. In this illumination she sees him and they share a farewell kiss. As Sam walks into the light he tells her that when you die you take the love that is inside with you. So there is little doubt that they will meet each other again in the Afterlife and be together forever.

↑

GHOST, THE MOVIE

Patrick Swayze as Sam Wheat is seen in this Ghost picture with Demi Moore as Molly Jensen. This classic fantasy love story has now reached a certain amount of cult status.

The Happy Hunting Grounds

 An eternity enjoying life after death in the peace and plenty of the Happy Hunting Grounds is a simplistic view of Native American traditions of the Afterlife. The real beliefs of Native Americans are far more complex and varied among the diverse tribes. Many tribes thought in terms of two souls, one of which remained with the body and perished, while the other was free to leave the body and explore— this was how a shaman might travel to the Otherworld, and how the worthy dead entered the Happy Hunting Grounds.

As with Western traditions, Native American legends also tell of Earthbound spirits—ghosts that need assistance or have a mission to fulfil before reaching their destined paradise.

TWO YOUNG FRIENDS
This Sioux legend tells of two young men who have been firm friends since childhood. One of them is chosen by the shaman's daughter to be her husband, but before marrying her he has to gain his feathers by defeating an enemy in battle. Although it is late in the year, the two friends set out together on the war path, traveling by foot toward the West, where their enemy's camps are most plentiful.

After ten days, after the two friends have entered their enemy's territory, a fierce snowstorm blows up. Rather than freeze in the open prairie the brave friends descend into the thickly wooded valley of the notorious Ghost Creek. There, the biting wind cannot reach them and they build a snug shelter from the snow, by bending the abundant willow branches into a dome and covering them like a tent.

As they eat their evening meal, a man slowly enters their tipi. They give him hospitality of food, drink, and a pipe to smoke. Then he speaks, telling them he is the ghost of a man of their own tribe who has been killed by their mutual enemy. He has been killed before he can begin to defend himself, so he has not died fighting as a warrior should and therefore can not enter the Happy Hunting Grounds. He is powerless to help himself and his salvation can only come from having the scalp of the man who has killed him.

The friends agree to help him and in return the ghost tells them how they can gain the honor they seek in combat and evade capture after killing their victims. The friends carry through the plan precisely, as agreed, taking the scalp that was asked for by the ghost and another scalp each to keep as trophies of their prowess as warriors. They give the cowardly killer's scalp to the ghost, who immediately disappears— bound for the Happy Hunting Grounds—and they go back to their tribe, where they are highly honored and the marriage ceremony quickly ensues.

THE GHOST BRIDE

The Pawnee tribe of Nebraska has a story of a young man who leaves his bride-to-be at his village while he goes with the men to hunt. While the hunters are away the young woman dies and the village packs up and follows the men on their seasonal migration. The young man returns to the village as soon as he can, without meeting the villagers or hearing of their sad news, and he travels alone.

When he arrives, the village is deserted, except for his bride-to-be. She explains that she's been depressed and sulky and has been content to be left behind for a while. They stay in the village that night, even though it is the custom for the ghosts of the tribe to visit the place when the people have moved away. The ghosts come dancing and singing from lodge to lodge, but the man stays with his girl all night.

In the morning they set off to rejoin their tribe, but the girl makes a strange request. She asks that he prepares a place for her to sleep, and that it is curtained off by day as well as by night for four whole days. Also, she says, he must not tell anyone who she is. She lingers behind as he goes into the new camp to make preparations.

When he has arranged her bed, he asks a female relative to fetch the girl. She is curious and asks who the girl is. The young man remembers not to mention her name, but names her parents. At this his relative is amazed and declares that the girl is dead. Try as they might, when they go to look for her, they cannot find the bride-to-be. If they had followed her plan for four days she would have lived again, but now she has vanished like the ghost she is. That night the groom-to-be dies in his sleep. Because the couple can not be together in his world, he follows her into hers.

THE LURE

Somewhere in Stanley Park, Vancouver, Canada is a stone containing the spirit of a woman whose heart was as hard-hearted and unyielding as the stone itself. She had been imprisoned at the command of the Great Spirit, as punishment for her wickedness. However, even now, anyone who comes too close to this white stone with black blotches, may yet fall victim to her dark magic. Once within range of her spirit, no human may escape, but is doomed to walk in circles around her. Even death cannot release her prey, for its spirit continues to tread its endless journey around her. For this reason she is known as The Lure.

The Great Spirit, in an attempt to prevent hapless and innocent people from stumbling accidentally on this terrible site, placed a stand of magnificent trees a safe distance away. These tall sentinels draw the eye from great distances and people flock to see them. Visitors wonder at their natural beauty as if in a living cathedral and do not feel the need to venture further, where they might fall into the fatal embrace of The Lure.

40 Great Ghost Movies

 The camera may never lie, but cinema certainly plays with the truth. Special effects and ghostly phenomena have always featured highly in movie entertainment. Here are 40 great ghost movies to look out for:

- *Ghost Rider* (2007)
- *White Noise* (2005)
- *The Haunted Mansion* (2003)
- *The Lord of the Rings: The Return of the King* (2003)
- *The Ring* (2002)
- *Harry Potter and the Philosopher's Stone* (2001)
- *Spirited Away* (2001)
- *The Others* (2001)
- *Thir13en Ghosts* (2001)
- *What Lies Beneath* (2000)
- *A Christmas Carol* (1999)
- *Scooby Doo and the Witch's Ghost* (1999)
- *Sixth Sense* (1999)
- *Sleepy Hollow* (1999)
- *Stir of Echoes* (1999)
- *The Haunting* (1999)
- *Titanic* (1997)
- *The Canterville Ghost* (1996)
- *The Frighteners* (1996)

- *Casper* (1995)
- *Haunted* (1995)
- *Bill & Ted's Bogus Journey* (1991)
- *Flatliners* (1990)
- *Ghost* (1990)
- *Eric the Viking* (1989)
- *Beetlejuice* (1988)
- *High Spirits* (1988)
- *Scrooged* (1988)
- *Ghostbusters* (1984)
- *Poltergeist* (1982)
- *An American Werewolf in London* (1981)
- *The Fog* (1980)
- *The Shining* (1980)
- *Kaidan* (1964)
- *The Haunting* (1963)
- *Carnival of Souls* (1962)
- *The Ghost and Mrs. Muir* (1947)
- *A Matter of Life & Death* (1946)
- *Blithe Spirit* (1945)
- *Topper* (1937)

BLITHE SPIRIT

In a scene from David Lean's 1945 *Blithe Spirit*, adapted from the play by Noel Coward, Kay Hammond appears as a ghost, eavesdropping on Rex Harrison's conversation with his new wife, Ruth Condomine.

Raising the Dead

TALKING WITH GHOSTS

Supernatural powers might be satisfying on their own account, but there are many practical reasons why we might wish to talk with ghosts. Discovering the secrets only the dead would know (such as who murdered them, where they put their will, or what it's like in the Afterlife) is a form of divination, and divination using the dead is called "necromancy." Nowadays, though, the word is usually reserved for summoning spirits against their will, and is regarded as a form of so-called Black Magic.

Communication

Modern mediums are not usually regarded as necromancers because they merely offer spirits an opportunity for communication, rather than compelling their attendance.

Perhaps the earliest description of a deliberate summoning of the dead occurs in Ancient Greek legend. Homer, who lived in the 8th century BCE and is the earliest-known Greek writer, gives us a vivid view of a ritual for raising the dead. It is thought to embody the beliefs current at the time.

THE "WITCH" OF ENDOR

In the 8th and 6th centuries BCE the Israelites made strenuous efforts to ban the practice of necromancy. This seems to indicate that it was fairly widespread at the time. One of these prohibitions—under pain of death—was issued by King Saul, who, ironically, actually resorted to a medium (frequently translated as "witch") to summon a ghost on his behalf.

Saul asked his attendants to find him a woman skilled in the art of necromancy and they suggested a medium at Endor. At night he went to her and asked her to raise a spirit—Samuel, a prophet of God. She did so (her method, unfortunately, is not recorded) and she saw the spirit of an old man, wearing a robe, come up from the ground.

At this point her clairvoyant powers awoke to the fact that her client was the king, but he granted her immunity from punishment for her services. Samuel addressed Saul, demanding the reason that he had been disturbed and brought up. Saul simply wanted some advice, but much to his disquiet, Samuel told him that God had turned against him and was now his enemy. Samuel added a prophecy that within a day both Saul and his sons would be with him in Sheol.

MEDIEVAL NECROMANCY

Perhaps because the souls of the Christian dead were supposed to be left in whatever peace God had granted them, anyone seeking to communicate with them would need to turn to the dark arts.

Ghosts in The Odyssey

The Odyssey tells the story of how Odysseus returned home on a ten-year journey after victory in the Trojan War. In books ten and eleven it describes the harrowing summoning of ghosts.

CONJURING SPIRITS

Circe, a beautiful goddess, gives Odysseus the details of a grisly rite to conjure the spirits of the dead, who can help him find his way home. She warns him only one ghost can help: an old prophet from Thebes, who has been allowed to keep his wits in the Underworld. All other ghosts are reduced to helpless shadows.

Odysseus and his crew sail to the land of perpetual mist on the border of Hades. Here they find a grove of willow and poplar trees, sacred to the goddess Persephone, queen of Hades. At a confluence of rivers, Odysseus digs a pit. Around this he pours three offerings to the dead: milk and honey, sweet wine, and water. Over these he sprinkles barley kernels.

CALLING THE DEAD

Odysseus calls the dead to come. Then he takes his sword and slits the throats of a ram and a ewe. As their bloods mingle, a multitude of ghosts rise up—brides, old men, warriors with battle wounds—and all are moaning. He then orders his men to skin and burn the carcasses of the sheep, while he guards the reeking pit with his sword. The first ghost is a member of Odysseus' own crew who has fallen to his death from a rooftop. He has reached Hades more quickly than the living crew, but Odysseus doesn't let him drink the blood. Then Odysseus' own mother draws near, but her eyes are on the blood and she doesn't recognize him. He doesn't let her drink. Then the blind prophet Teiresias comes and offers help in return for drinking the blood. Odysseus withdraws his sword and the ghost drinks deeply. True to his word, the Egyptian foretells the route the hero would take to reach home. And, when questioned about why Odysseus' mother failed to recognize him, Teiresias explains that only by drinking the blood can a ghost's rational mind be roused. Without this sustenance, the ghosts remain shadows and eventually withdraw. Now sated, Teiresias himself withdraws.

EMPTY EMBRACES

Odysseus' mother returns and drinks and Odysseus tries to hug her three times, but she slips through his arms. She explains that at death the soul leaves the body, like a dream, to flutter in the air. When she departs, Persephone wills that all the royal daughters and wives should drink and they throng around Odysseus. But he holds them back until they tell him their stories of honor, treachery, love, and vengeance. Then the men arrive.

Odysseus also sees the ghost of the hunter Orion, herding the ghosts of animals he's slain in life. He sees Tantalus, too, doomed to stand in a pool of water that disappears whenever he stoops to slake his thirst, while above him luscious fruits are blown away by the wind whenever he tries to reach them. As all the other ghosts of men swarm around him, Odysseus finally loses his nerve and flees for safety, leaving the bloody pit to the horde of hungry spirits.

Murmur, the demon

In 1577 the Dutch physician and occultist Johann Weyer published the *Pseudomonarchia Daemonum* (False Kingdom of Demons), which names more than 60 demons that could grant requests specific to their nature.

One of these demons, Murmur, not only teaches philosophy but, at the magician's request, brings the souls of the dead to answer questions. Murmur is a middle-ranking demon in the infernal hierarchy, and will arrive preceded by heralds blowing trumpets. He will be further recognizable dressed as a soldier and riding on a griffin—a composite creature combining the body of a lion with the head and wings of an eagle. These demons, with a few more added, now totaling 72, also appear in the 17th-century grimoire *Ars Goetia* (Arts of Sorcery). Here, each demon has a unique seal or symbol that the magician can use to conjure the spirit. The seal of Murmur is made of copper (see above right).

The ceremony for evoking such demons was long and arduous, as the demons were almost always busy with diabolical works, and their nature was inherently rebellious. They would not readily answer the magician's summons.

ELIPHAS LÉVI

Summoning the dead was a little easier by the 19th century, when French magician Eliphas Lévi devoted a chapter of his *Dogma et Rituel de la Haute Magie (The Dogma and Ritual of Transcendental Magic)* to necromancy. In this work he explains that to see and communicate

SEAL OF MURMUR

This copper seal is used by the magician to conjure up the spirit. Murmur is a Great Duke and Earl of Hell and has a grand total of 30 legions of demons beneath his command.

CHILD OF EARTH

Eliphas Lévi created this composite figure as a symbol of the human condition—part animal and part spiritual, powerful yet merciful, illuminated by the fire of reason (from *The Dogma and Ritual of Transcendental Magic*.)

SOLVE

COAGULA

ELIPHAS LEVI DEL.

The House of Hel

 The *Poetic Edda* is a collection of Norse myths and legends of heroes. It includes a story called *Balder's Dream (Baldrs Draumar)*, written in Icelandic at the start of the 14th century CE. This myth tells of the happy and beautiful god, Balder, who becomes plagued by ominous dreams. This so upsets the whole company of gods that they convene to help him, but no cure is found. Then Odin—the chief of the gods, and the God of Magic— rises and saddles his eight-legged horse Sleipnir. He rides to the realm of the goddess Hel, which is populated by the ghosts of the unhappy dead.

On his journey Odin encounters the hound that comes up from Hel's depths to challenge him. The hound howls fearfully, its breast covered in the blood of the dead, but Odin continues undaunted. Reaching the high house of Hel, Odin rides to the eastern door and there he stops. At the grave of a wise woman, who was a seer and a mother of giants, Odin speaks the magic spells that bind her, and raises her from the dead.

Odin proceeds to question her. After each of her replies she says her answer was forced from her, and now it is her desire to be still. But he relentlessly counters that she must continue to speak until he knows all he wishes to learn. This question and answer continues until Odin learns the reason for Balder's troubling dreams. He continues pressing for more details, however, until she realizes that she has been spellbound by him. As soon as she knows his name she is freed from his enchantment and tells him that she will answer no more until such time as the gods are destroyed. With this bleak but forceful prophesy, the poem ends.

with the spirits of the dead the magician must induce in him- or herself a state of trance-like lucid sleepwalking. However, even then, he asserts, we would not be able to commune with the true soul of the person, which would have ascended to Heaven already, but only with the astral body that is left alive but gradually dissolving in the astral light.

Using the pentagram
In 1854 Lévi himself tried to conjure the ghost of the famous ancient sage Apollonius of Tyana. In the ritual he used a gilded pentagram engraved on an altar of white marble, encircled by a chain of magnetized iron, and surrounded by four concave mirrors. He wore a white robe with a crown of gold woven with vervain leaves, and

Apprenticed to a Ghost

Sometimes we can learn from ghosts without even trying. There are lessons we might all learn, such as moral lessons about wrong-doing and remorse, or the wonder and power of love; but some people find ghosts helpful in other, quite specific, ways.

The ancient market town of Totnes, Devon, UK, has a neighborhood called Bridgend, which has an old blacksmith's forge, whose origins may be medieval. When tractors began to replace horse power, demand everywhere for the smithy waned, and this old forge closed in 1948. In due course it was bought by the Allnutt family, who ran the house as a hotel and reopened the blacksmith's forge as a modern business specializing in wrought-iron work

Guests at the hotel often praised Mrs. Allnutt for her husband's industry, saying they could hear the faint but unmistakable sounds of the blacksmith's hammer working on the anvil all night. But the smithy had been locked and empty. Suspicions that a blacksmith from the past still pursued the labor he loved were

confirmed when Mr. Allnutt received his first commission—he was presented with a damaged sword for repair. While the metalwork posed no particular difficulties, the sword had a jewel-encrusted hilt and Mr. Allnutt was worried about the heat from the forge damaging the stones. He put the sword aside while he tried to find out how best to approach the job—the best thing he could have done, because he awoke one morning with the procedure absolutely clear in his mind.

Some people might put this down to the power of the subconscious, well known for working out problems in our dreams (the advice to "sleep on it" is not just a way of putting things off.) But Mr. Allnutt was adamant that the solution was given to him by the old smith, whose spirit had been haunting the forge. This relationship continued, with the master smith giving advice from his lifetime's experience. Mr. Allnutt often felt his hands being guided by the spirit, until 1991, when it seems his apprenticeship was completed and the spirit moved on, leaving the forge in trusted hands.

as he burned various incenses he saw in the smoke the figure he was seeking.

Despite receiving answers to his questions, Lévi remained sceptical that the figure was actually the ghost of Apollonius. He stated that the ritual was designed to produce a sort of drunkenness of the imagination and contented himself with

the conclusion that the ritual had successfully achieved this.

The effects of grief
An altered state of consciousness may also be induced by grief. Yearning for the loved one, we lose sleep and fail to eat. If we then see their ghost, it may be a hallucination (as Lévi suggests.)

Ghostly Experiences

Poltergeists are spirits that make their presence known by moving objects around, even throwing them, and making noises. They also specialize in acts of mischief. The great majority of poltergeist cases seem to revolve around a living person, typically a teenage girl, and such phenomena are regarded as recurrent spontaneous psychokinesis (RSPK). Psychokinesis (PK) is the alleged power of the human mind to move things, by deliberate effort of will. It is this ability that manifests in a random and uncontrolled way, during a poltergeist outbreak.

POLTERGEISTS AT THE GEORGE INN

Not all poltergeists are terrifying and although their name means "noisy ghost" in German, some play pranks that are so gentle we can easily accept them, especially if life is a little dull.

Perhaps it is the slow pace of life in the countryside that mellowed the poltergeist at the George Inn, Blackawton, Devon, UK. This poltergeist had seen numerous landlords come and go, with reports of paranormal activity stretching back for half a century.

Tracey and Bob Clark took over the pub in 2006 and lived upstairs with their teenaged son, Curtis. They soon began to notice paranormal phenomena. Scampering footsteps were heard on the first floor, door handles would be rattled at night and sometimes the doors opened, though

no one was there. In the bathroom, the cold tap turned itself on. Tracey wasn't fazed and said out loud "Can you turn that off please?" and the water stopped running.

Pennies and two-pence coins began to turn up in the shower. At first Tracey wondered whether she had dropped them herself, but then wondered why she would have money on her in the shower. But when this became a regular occurrence she could no longer laugh it off.

Who you gonna call?

When a chance remark put her in touch with Hidden Realms, a local paranormal investigation team, they embarked on a detailed investigation to get to the bottom of the disturbance. Methods employed included mediums, a survey of the house and its history, a psychic artist, a psychometrist, and dowsers. Hidden Realms

---

POLTERGEIST DRAMA

This old illustration shows typical poltergeist activity: a whole range of household equipment seems to be flying about by itself, around the focal point of a young person or child, in this case a baby in a cradle.

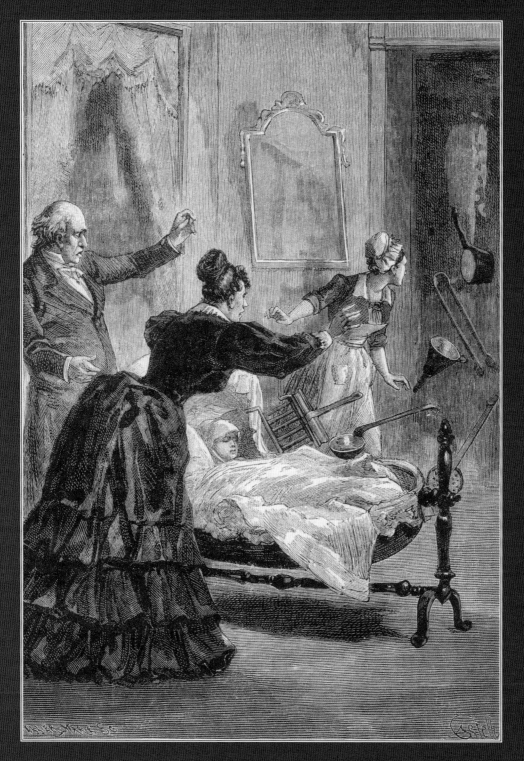

held a vigil and their equipment included a beam-break motion detector, a locked-off video camera, and a digital audio recorder, but nothing extraordinary was recorded. The team's sensitives, however, found much to say. They described a lynching dating to 1747 in which Abigail was falsely accused of a crime, by Josey, a beautiful yet flawed woman who still haunts the bar.

The trial was held upstairs, and Abigail's lover, George Baker, tried to reach her to break it up. But he was intercepted by a mob that attacked him with pitchforks and knives, in the field at the rear of the pub. They buried his body in an unmarked grave in unhallowed ground and innocent Abigail was taken away and hanged. The sensitive sensed that the man's spirit was still crying out with the distraught message "Tell her I did all I could."

One night, Hidden Realms left a sound recorder on all night in the downstairs passage between the two bars. This recorded a number of knocks, taps, and scrapes, and a noise that sounded like a buzzing mosquito, but which some thought was a voice saying "hello" or "help."

Dark shadow of ghostly monks

Ghostly monks have been seen in the George Inn for half a century at least. Kathie Langford worked as a barmaid in the 1960s and often saw a solitary figure of a hooded man, both at night and in the day. Once she was in the lounge with the landlord and a customer, when all three of them noticed somebody walking across the room. The startled customer said "Did you see that?" And the landlord matter-of-factly pronounced that they'd just seen "Fred," as the mysterious monk was commonly called.

THE GEORGE INN

Focus of ghostly activity, especially poltergeist, this atmospheric old country inn has been the subject of much activity during the recent past. But no one has ever been quite able to get to the bottom of it.

Tracey's Poltergeist Diary (January 2008)

It was suggested that Tracey keep a diary of all the unexplained activity in her home. In a single month, she listed the following occurrences:

→ *Knocks were heard on the bedroom doors, but nobody was there.*

→ *Doors opened on their own.*

→ *A light turned on by itself.*

→ *A bell rang in an unoccupied area of the bar.*

→ *A shoe levitated briefly.*

→ *A hi-fi cable disappeared, only to reappear at a place already searched.*

→ *A can of polish leaped from a table.*

→ *An iPod turned on in an unoccupied bedroom.*

→ *A full bottle of brandy disappeared and was found behind a TV set.*

History tells us that by 1258 the feudal lord of Blackawton had given his manor to the Premonstratensian monastery of Torre Abbey. This established a strong ecclesiastical influence in the area. The monastery was home to canons who lived by monastic rule and people had always assumed this connection explains the stories of ghostly monks. But the Premonstratensian canons were commonly known as White Canons because of their light-colored habits, so the dark figures haunting the George are certainly not the ghosts of these historical priests.

However, there was nothing dim or hazy about the three monks seen by Tracey. They strolled serenely along the first-floor corridor, as large as life and in the middle of the day. Perhaps there actually were monks at the site after all.

Dowsing for evidence

The Society of Moorland Dowsers responded to an invitation to visit. Set up in 1993, this group of specialists is recognized as an authority in dowsing lost, ancient buildings and associated energy lines.

Three dowsers arrived on a rainy day and their professionalism shone through as they dowsed the George—indoors and out. Using two metal rods (one in each hand), held horizontally, that crossed or parted to indicate answers to questions, the dowsers not only attempted to assess the archeology of the site, but also sought to discover the details of spirits from centuries past. Their combination of talents enabled them to survey what they said was the first building erected on the site of the George: an abbey barn.

Psychic Art and Automatic Writing

In January 2008 psychic artist Dawn Lodge visited the George Inn at the invitation of Hidden Realms. She sensed "that it wasn't always a pub, that it was something like a nursing home." Upstairs, she drew the portrait of the woman, while the man was drawn downstairs.

"I had a feeling they were looking after people. There was a caring feeling about the place. I sensed children. I had the feeling that the lady was more in charge. She was the one that did most of the caring. She was no fool, a spade was a spade. A very strong woman, but very caring.

"I feel they lived there, and I think they were 'attached.' He was a jokey, 'laid-back' gentleman—good company and he kept everybody in high spirits. He was more of a helper. I suppose with what she had to do he was more the backbone or support. It was a very interesting night."

Another interesting night at the George Inn saw some of the Hidden Realms team conduct an experiment in automatic writing. Kim produced what appears to be a name, "Churchman." It is an unusual surname that does exist in Devon, but is not known to occur in Blackawton itself. However, it may not be a name but a description—a "man of the church."

Above: *"Churchman," an example of automatic writing carried out at the George Inn.*

Near and far left: *The man and woman drawn by psychic artist Dawn Lodge at the George Inn. She felt they were caring people.*

Psychometry on an Apport

 One Wednesday evening around 10 p.m., Curtis, the teenaged son of the landlord, went to close the door at the foot of the stairs (which lead up to the family's living rooms.) "As he did so," Tracey told me, "he noticed a two-pence coin bouncing down the stairs toward him! It came all the way down and landed in the bar." She added "No one was upstairs, not even the cat."

This coin was an "apport," a word brought into usage in the late 19th century to describe events in seances where objects appear from nowhere. It was taken to psychic medium Tony Stockwell to see what psychometry could offer. He said the energy from the coin made his hand and arm tingle strongly and added that the apport was sent as a means of communication by the spirit of a young woman with very dark hair.

The Hidden Realms team noted that this description fitted Josey very well, although they had always assumed it was William who had been flinging money around. The coin, incidentally, was dated 1980 and in unusually good condition, as if it had been out of circulation for much of that time.

This was a sort of ecclesiastical warehouse used for collecting and storing the agricultural produce of the manor, which belonged to the abbey. Built around the middle of the 14th century, they said the barn was a thatched, stone structure, and slightly larger than the present building.

One dowser mentioned the suspected murder at the site and another used the rods to determine that seven people were in the mob, and that the attack occurred in 1546. This date is at odds with that obtained by Hidden Realms' own sensitives, who put the event a full two centuries later.

Afterword

Although it is well known that poltergeists are associated with the presence of a young person, Tracey reports that since leaving the George Inn, they have experienced no poltergeist phenomena at all. This indicates that it was the site rather than anyone in the family that was the focus for the haunting. This is unusual, as an estimated 75 percent of poltergeists are thought to be associated with people, most frequently girls or women under the age of 20.

Trouble in the Barn

 The Haunted is a TV series featuring a wide variety of cases involving animals in a ten-part series launched in 2009. Stories include the strange case involving horses at a sanctuary in Barkhamsted, Connecticut, USA, that were being mysteriously moved in their stalls at night. The owners suspected that youngsters might be playing a prank, so they tied string to the barn doors and pieces of tape on the windows, hoping to reveal how the intruders were getting into the building. But in the morning all the traps were still in place, yet again the horses had been moved. Other phenomena that had occurred in the ten years since the family moved in included bridles that disappeared only to turn up later. The ghost of a man wearing overalls was frequently seen near the barn, and a 19th-century soldier appeared in the house beside the fireplace. The scent of floral perfume would sometimes mysteriously manifest, while at other times it would be the smell of burning pipe tobacco.

In the summer of 2008 the owners called Northwest Connecticut Paranormal Society for help. The society was founded by John and Mandi Zontok in 2004 to conduct research in a sceptical way and to help educate the public. They have conducted hundreds of onsite investigations. Other episodes of *The Haunted* feature the ghosts of animals themselves, such as the spirits of monkeys heard growling and seen haunting the Candle Shoppe of the Poconos in Swiftwater, Pennsylvania.

EVP (electronic voice phenomena, recordings of anomalous sounds) provided some impressive evidence of paranormal activity. In one of these, Mandi was alone in the barn when something scared the horses. She asked "Did you just scare the horses?" To which a male voice replied with a hastily whispered "Sorry."

One of the team was animal psychic Traci Shannon, who managed to engage with the ghost, who she believes is a former owner, and helped him to cross over. Since then the society has heard of no further disturbances. An investigation carried out by the Pennsylvania Paranormal Association revealed that early in the 20th century a scientist had conducted animal experiments there. He used the primates for medical research by infecting them, and although the investigation was inconclusive, the team felt there was sufficient evidence to warrant a return visit. The owners simply wanted the unquiet spirits laid to rest.

Craig-y-nos Castle

 This Welsh neo-gothic castle was built in the 1840s by a wealthy businessman as his family home and was bought by famous opera singer Adelina Patti, who installed a theatre seating 150 people, which opened in 1891.

When Caroline Johnson stayed at the castle on the night of 12 August 2004, she shared a twin bedroom with her friend Lyn Cinderley. This was located in what were once the theatre's changing rooms. After a tour of the castle, the two of them retired for the night, Caroline taking the bed nearest the door. The beds had been made up with sheets and quilts, but the August night was warm, even with the window open, so they consigned the quilts to the floor and slept comfortably with just the sheets.

Caroline, who is sensitive to things of the spirit world, woke first, soon after sunrise, and was instantly aware they weren't alone in the room. She was lying on her front and she intuited the presence of a woman, a nurse.

Caroline related "The woman walked around to the foot of my bed and observed me for a few seconds and I thought that would be it, but instead she tugged at my sheet, which was covering me and had tucked it under my arm. I tugged back, as if to say 'I'm not having that!' and the reply was a double tug as if to say 'Come on stop playing around.' I released my grip and the sheet slid out of my hand. I lay there frozen to the spot as she tucked me in, even picking up the quilt and placing that over me and tucking in the edges, yet I felt calm and reassured that I could see this caring nurse.

"She then sat on the end of the bed and watched me before getting up and walking over to Lyn's bed. By now I was going through a mix of excitement and pure fear, but I had to overcome my fear. I could see Lyn and the sheets were actually lifting and moving! I watched the nurse tuck her in and again sit on the bed, which actually woke Lyn momentarily, but she turned over and went back to sleep. The nurse calmly and quietly walked out of the bedroom."

Caroline later heard that several other people had felt themselves being tucked in at night, in a different part of the castle. And the owner confirmed that both rooms were in fact used as wards when the site became a Children's Tuberculosis Sanatorium (1922 to 1959) after Madame Patti died.

Comptez sur lui pour vous empoisonner la mort

Michael Keaton est

BEETLEJUICE

Même les fantômes n'en veulent plus.

BEETLEJUICE, THE MOVIE, 1988

The mischievous ghost Beetlejuice (Michael Keaton) claims to be a bio-exorcist and is hired by newly dead couple Barbara (Geena Davis) and Adam Maitland (Alec Baldwin) to scare the new owners out of their house. This is a poster from this classic supernatural comedy by director Tim Burton.

POLTERGEIST ACTIVITY

Perhaps objects start floating around and eerie noises howl through the house, but the poltergeist behind phenomena might not necessarily be evil; perhaps it simply doesn't like sharing its home. The Oscar-winning comedy *Beetlejuice* (1988) shows what difficulties even the most mild-mannered ghosts face when trying to communicate with the people who move into their home. It also shows that, with a little give and take, even the most unlikely combinations of living and dead can learn to get along happily together, as is the case in the poignant tale from the Scottish Highlands (see box right).

POSSESSION

Horror movies have made us very aware of the dangers of becoming possessed by demons: *The Exorcist* movie is the prime example of this genre. But occasionally people claim to be possessed by a ghost. Unlike demonic possession, which is frequently found in movies, overt possession by a ghost is a rare phenomenon. Perhaps the main reason for this is that ghostly possessions are complex and cerebral because the incoming ghost would require adroit psychological counseling on the morality of their actions.

A demon, on the other hand, is met bluntly with extreme prejudice, in a battle where all hell breaks loose. Few real-life ghostly possessions are reported because first, the possessing ghost would be expected to give verifiable information about its past life; and because second, the church that carries out the exorcisms believes such spirits are actually demons trying to confuse us. Many movies do include an occasional scene involving possession by ghosts, but these are usually in comic situations.

The Colquhonnie Poltergeist

A WOMAN WRONGED

Nestling in the beautiful foothills of Scotland's Cairngorm Mountains, the 220-year-old Colquhonnie Hotel, Strathdon, was home to an unhappy spirit.

Sally and John Wright, who ran the hotel in the early 2000s, told me of some guests from New Zealand who had asked them about a lady they'd seen wearing an old-fashioned outfit of a dark green, ankle-length skirt and a white, high-collared blouse. They had spotted her through their camera lens. The Wrights knew nothing about her, but later a local resident said he'd seen her on numerous occasions. The current owner, Paul MacLennan, became increasingly perplexed by mysterious disturbances, which he said were prevalent when he was renovating. These included temperature drops and glasses being thrown about. Once Paul was tapped on the shoulder and another time a loud clattering was heard in the dining room in the dead of night. A complete place setting had been laid—with knives, forks, spoons, plates, and a napkin all ready and awaiting a single diner—on the floor. Such phenomena are often attention-seeking behaviors; the frustrated outbursts of ghosts who feel ignored or slighted. Eventually Paul contacted a minister at a Roman Catholic cathedral, who agreed to perform an exorcism. He took photographs of the bars and the dining room. One of these showed a lady wearing an ankle-length skirt and a white, high-collared blouse. Investigation of old records reveal a young woman working at the hotel at around the turn of the 20th century, who suffered an attempted assault by a drunken man. As she fled his unwelcome embrace she fell down some steps. Tragically, although she saved her honor, she broke her neck and died.

IMPROVED ATMOSPHERE

Following the exorcism, Paul noticed that the atmosphere changed dramatically, becoming serene and calm. He feels that the ghostly lady is still around, though, but it's likely that she no longer feels compelled to use poltergeist tactics just to be noticed. She has clearly found she can live in peace with her living co-workers and they are at home with their resident ghost. Sally further informed me that the name Colquhonnie means "the back place of weeping." This evocative name comes from the local tradition that the mournful sound of bagpipes played here could be heard for miles along the valley. The soulful piper that plays in this tranquil site could scarcely be further removed from the sinister spirit of the piper in our next tale.

The Piper—Herald of Death

 The case of the piper, first published in 1911, demonstrates how a situation can degenerate into insanity. The scene of the tragedy was a 16th-century building, now demolished, called Donalgowerie House, on the outskirts of Perth, Scotland.

The Whittingen family, consisting of a retired gentleman, his wife, and their five grown-up children, bought and moved into the property one June, and it was in September of that year that the first terrifying incident occurred. The day that ended under a supernatural shadow had begun in the brilliance of celebrations for the marriage of one of Mr. Whittingen's sons.

In the party atmosphere, the three daughters naturally received attention from the eligible bachelors of the county. Following a brisk game of croquet, one of the young men asked to see some of the photographs Mary had taken. Flattered, she obligingly retired to her bedroom to find her album.

In the garden Martha was also enjoying the company of the young suitors, but was eventually persuaded to try and find out why Mary had failed to return from her room. Irritated at having to leave her flirtations, Martha quickly went up to the upper storey of the house and arrived on the long, dark corridor that led to Mary's room.

There, though, she stopped in her tracks. Coming out of Mary's open door was a man wearing a kilt and carrying bagpipes under his arm. He glided silently toward her in such an unearthly way that Martha could not utter a sound. His face was an ashen grey and his eyes were fierce with menace. But still she could not move. Neither did he stop. He passed right through her and disappeared through a window behind her that led to a sheer drop.

Recovering her wits, Martha ran to the bedroom to find Mary. She was lying on the floor in a dead faint. When she came to her senses she demanded to know who had let the piper in. He had, she said, appeared out of nowhere, fixed her with his malevolent gaze, laid his icy hand on her shoulder for a moment, and then started pacing up and down playing a dirge on his bagpipes. His actions so resembled those of a madman that Mary assumed he would turn and murder her, and it was then that she had fallen into unconsciousness.

Exactly a week later Mary met with a freak accident on the croquet lawn, cut her head, and developed blood poisoning. She died within a fortnight. Martha had no doubt that the piper had somehow heralded her death.

One Sunday shortly before Christmas, the family were sitting in the drawing room after tea, when they heard the sound of a horse-drawn carriage approach the house at speed. Although the knocks on the front door were abnormally loud, no servant ventured to open it. Yet the door did open and heavy footfalls echoed through the house as the unknown guests came toward the drawing room.

Martha darted to the door and locked it, but it opened to them regardless, and a group of ghostly figures entered the room. Ruth, the third of the daughters, fainted. The ghosts turned abruptly about and left as they had arrived, leaving a violent wind in their wake, an icy blast that chilled the soul.

When Ruth regained consciousness, she declared that they had come for her, and that she would die soon, like Mary. Within two weeks she developed appendicitis and, despite the best of care, she died.

THE PIPER RETURNS
A full year passed without incident and with the arrival of Easter came a return visit from the married son and his wife, this time bringing their baby son. During their stay a day came when everyone was away from the house either on business or enjoying a pleasant day out, everyone except the baby and Martha, who stayed to look after him. As the sun set, Martha gazed out from her upstairs window. A noise behind her startled her. Still haunted by her fear of the ghosts that had visited the house, she looked around the room, hunting for the cause of the sound. Her eyes came to rest on a shawl left behind by the baby's nurse. As she moved

toward it her eyes became fixed on the pair of scissors beside it. As she picked them up she felt something snake around her waist. In an instant she looked down she saw the livid face of the piper gazing up into her eyes. His arm was around her, guiding her toward the cot. Her will was eclipsed by the force of his evil intent. It was her hand that took the sharp blades to the baby's soft skin, but it was not her doing. She was possessed.

After the act, the piper struck up his mournful dirge on the pipes, and backed away in solemn, despicable triumph. With his disappearance, Martha's wits returned, and the sight of the crimson blood on the white sheets sent her into a shrieking madness, from which she never fully recovered. She died soon after, broken in spirit. Her parents quickly sold the old house, which was demolished.

Such ghost stories nowadays are almost unheard of. Medical advances and the lifting of mental illness out of the underworld of stigma mean that relatively few troubled minds are left to battle evil impulses alone. But the would-be paranormal investigator should remember that not all people are friendly and honest and anecdotal evidence firmly suggests ghosts retain much of the personality they had in life. When we look for ghosts we may find them—warts and all.

Ten Best-known Hauntings

 The following selection of stories are among the best-known hauntings:

AMITYVILLE, LONG ISLAND, USA
Menacing phenomena in the 1970s included apparitions of hooded figures, disembodied voices, mysterious stenches, insect infestations, and walls dripping with slime. Despite accusations of it being a hoax, several successful movies were inspired by the book *The Amityville Horror.*

BACHELOR'S GROVE CEMETERY, ILLINOIS, USA
Having fallen into disuse in the 1980s, this is now claimed to be among the most haunted cemeteries in the world. Sightings include the Madonna, otherwise known as the "white lady," who is seen on full-moon nights wandering with a baby in her arms; a man with two heads; and a large, white house complete with veranda, which appears in different places.

BLOODY MARY
Known in various places, this spirit may be summoned by gazing into a mirror at midnight in a room lit by a single candle, and saying her name three times. Her arrival, though, is to be feared. Whoever calls her forth is either driven insane, or she claws out their eyes, or she pulls them bodily into the mirror.

BORLEY RECTORY, ESSEX, UK
Among the most studied haunted sites in the world, this building was burned down in 1939. Phenomena included a ghostly nun, a coach and horses, mysterious voices, and poltergeist activity ranging from writing on walls to showers of pebbles and glass bottles appearing from nowhere. Activity continued in the ruins.

EPWORTH HOUSE, LINCOLNSHIRE, UK
Poltergeist activity flared up in December 1716 and January 1717 and it was recorded in contemporary letters, providing details of phenomena that included groans, knocking, running footsteps, rumblings, rattling metal, and the sounds of smashing glass. Ghostly animal and human figures were also seen in this, the family home of famous Methodist, John Wesley.

FLIGHT 401, FLORIDA, USA
When a passenger plane crashed in the Florida Everglades in 1972, with great loss of life, the captain and his second officer apparently undertook to safeguard other flights from similar tragedy. Their spirits have been seen many times aboard aircraft, always vigilant to prevent mishap.

MYRTLES PLANTATION, LOUISIANA, USA
Spirits include William Winter, murdered in 1871, several union soldiers, a young girl, and Chloe, a slave sexually abused by her master in

the early 1800s. The story alleges she attempted to poison him after he cut off one of her ears, but killed his wife and children instead. Her spirit wears the green turban she wore to hide her disfigurement.

PHILIP, TORONTO, CANADA

In 1972 the Toronto Society for Psychical Research began an experiment to create a ghost. They named it Philip and invented a comprehensive back-story for him. When they asked him to communicate, they experienced phenomena that has been assumed to be psychokinetic, including rapping sounds, a levitating table, and cool breezes.

TOWER OF LONDON, LONDON, UK

Many ghosts cluster in this eleventh-century castle. These include King Henry VI and two princes, one of whom was the uncrowned king Edward V. Guy Fawkes groans endlessly and Sir Walter Raleigh also walks here, as does doomed queen Anne Boleyn and the Countess of Salisbury (both executed by Henry VIII), the latter still fleeing the executioner's axe.

WINCHESTER MYSTERY HOUSE, CALIFORNIA, USA

Work on this bizarre mansion began in 1884, commissioned by the eccentric heiress Sarah Winchester, who inherited a fortune earned from the famous Winchester rifle. It is said that a medium told her the souls of those killed by the weapon demanded a home. So she built the house to accommodate them all, continually adding to it until her death in 1922.

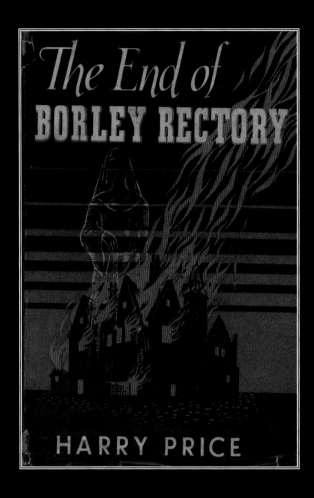

BORLEY RECTORY

First published in 1946, *The End of Borley Rectory* is by Harry Price, who had studied the haunting for years. However, its value as a reliable account has been challenged by sceptics, who mistrust Price's methods for gathering information.

4

Ghost-hunting

Quest for the Paranormal

There are few things as exciting as investigating ghosts, which are among life's great mysteries. And unlike other fields, where advances need complex equipment, in paranormal investigation all we really need is ourselves. Many people have taken these first steps before and their journeys have taken them in many different directions. Some end up with opinions opposite to the ones they started off with and many researchers look at the same experiences in opposing ways.

TRUST YOURSELF!

When conducting this kind of research, we need to learn to trust ourselves—not as easy as it sounds. We're forever failing to live up to our own aspirations and we're also rather easily fooled. But as long as we carry a spark of independence we can learn from mistakes and make real progress. Some researchers spend their lives in academic study and conduct exquisitely controlled experiments, while others enjoy the rough and tumble of research in the field and confront the unexpected in challenging situations. Both specialists and generalists are needed and to achieve success in either takes careful attention to detail, a determination to take the next step, and a good deal of luck. In short, we need our wits about us. The quest for the paranormal is a strange adventure and there are potential dangers. Some of us face these alone; others prefer the companionship of a group, but either way, encounters with the unknown will affect us profoundly and give us experiences we'll remember for the rest of our lives.

Ghost detectors

There is a bewildering variety of electronic detectors on the market and buying enough equipment to set up a comprehensive grid in a reputedly haunted house could cost as much as the house itself. Some groups, such as The Atlantic Paranormal Society, which features in the 2004 American reality TV series *Ghost Hunters* and *Ghost Hunters International*, focus on the scientific investigation of hauntings and instruments to gather empirical evidence. Recording devices may capture events beyond the range of human senses, but they have yet to provide unequivocal proof of the existence of ghosts. High-tech gadgets seem better at showing us what ghosts are not, rather than what they are. Most groups agree the only really essential piece of kit is free—ourselves.

GHOST HUNTERS

Grant Wilson and Jason Hawes get to grips with their mission in Season Two, screened in 2004. Deciding how to deploy an arsenal of ghost-hunting gadgets is a real test of our tactical abilities.

Preparing for a Vigil

ADVANCE PREPARATIONS

The mind and senses can and will play tricks when you put yourself into a spooky environment, so before you encounter a potentially dangerous interactive ghost, you need to learn to recognize these natural effects. This is an exciting process of self-discovery and its importance cannot be stressed too highly.

The safest place to become familiar with these effects is probably in the comfort of the home. If a haunted location is required, don't risk tangling with an interactive ghost, but select one where a ghostly event is replayed like a recording, the same way every time (see pages 56–62).

Even from the beginning you should not see this visit as a single opportunity, but rather approach it with the idea that you can return. You may wish to check findings, search for mundane causes for phenomena, or simply come back to find out more. This sort of investigation is known as a "longitudinal investigation," and can be far more revealing than a one-off visit.

RESEARCHING SITE HISTORY

Every historian knows the difference between a primary source and a secondary source, but few paranormal investigators are trained historians. However, knowing one from the other can make all the difference in the world.

Ghost-Hunting Checklist

Your kit should include...

- → Sandwiches and chocolate for instant energy.
- → Water, a flask of hot drink, fruit juice.
- → Warm clothes with a hat, scarf, gloves, etc.
- → Torch with good-quality spare batteries.
- → Notebook for writing and sketching.
- → Fully charged mobile phone.
- → Watch, to note the time events occur.
- → Camera and sound recorder to back up to your memory of events.

Always...

- → Choose your site carefully—it should be free from disturbance.
- → Get permission—have your visit authorized by the site owner.
- → Create a site dossier—compile a history of the location and its paranormal phenomena.
- → Respect health and safety—write a list of all potential hazards at the site.
- → Take emergency contacts—who to call if anything goes wrong.

The Site Report

 It is customary to give the owner of the site a written report of the investigation. When you first contact them, ask what level of privacy they prefer (at some point you may wish to publish findings.) The same applies to photographs. While a verbal agreement is often forthcoming, it is best to have confirmation in writing, ideally with a signature. Make a similar arrangement with team members. The site report usually includes the site history, especially its paranormal activity. It also features quotes from investigators' journals. The concluding paragraphs are usually added after the debriefing (normally held after the investigation.) The final version of the report should be given to the site owner and all members of the team. Ideally it should also be made accessible to reputable researchers interested in this field. Many paranormal investigation groups have websites and publish reports online, which means care needs to be taken regarding personal details.

Paranormal Site Investigators are recognized as one of the leading field-research teams and employ the scientific method both to approach investigations and analyze their results. In America, the Rhode Island Society for the Examination of Unusual Phenomena has a website with helpful articles and some investigation cases, as does Ghost Research International in Australia.

Primary and secondary

Primary sources are generally created at, or very close to, the events they describe and may be termed an "insider's view."

Secondary sources tend to be a retelling of events based on primary sources. The difference between the two may clearly be seen in the relationship between notes taken during a vigil and the site report. The report is based on the notes, so the notes are the primary source and the report secondary.

Manipulation of sources

Electronic voice phenomena recordings and photographs taken during a vigil are primary sources and remain so even if they are embedded inside a secondary source such as a website. However, if the EVP recordings or photos have been manipulated to enhance audio or optical clarity, these versions are secondary sources—derived from the original. When you research traditional ghost stories you should always check sources. It takes time, but it gives a deeper understanding of the case.

Ghost-hunting Gadgets

EQUIPMENT TO TAKE ALONG

Perhaps the most important equipment to take is also the cheapest—pen and paper. The sooner you write down an experience the better (this is the primary source, remember). Do this even before you start talking it over with other people.

Recording detail

Write down the event in as much detail as possible. You can always edit bits out when you write the report, but you can't add them in without risking false memories (such as helpful suggestions from other witnesses or people you've spoken to) and simple mistakes contaminating the narrative. A factual record written on the spot, with the possibility that further phenomena could occur at any second, will convey the authentic atmosphere in a direct way that cannot be replicated later.

Your journal should also record times when people move between locations. Taken together, the team's journals should show where everyone is at any moment. This can be invaluable in sourcing noises, as they may be traced back to somebody in an adjoining room; they may even establish that human activity can be ruled out.

Just as electric batteries are drained by low temperatures, some pens seize up when it gets cold, so either find a brand you can trust or take a pencil as a backup.

Walkie-talkies

These are useful for keeping track of everyone's movements during the investigation, as well as to summon other team members to witness phenomena, or in emergencies.

Analysis bags

Clean, self-sealing plastic bags and small bottles are useful just in case small objects or liquids are found that need to be brought back for analysis.

Cameras

The all-time favorite piece of ghost-hunting kit is the camera. There are, of course, significant technical differences between film and digital cameras, and many groups take both, to give themselves the best chance of capturing evidence. Video cameras are also very popular with investigators, particularly as they can monitor a site without needing anyone to be physically present. This both frees people to do more useful tasks and prevents human error or deliberate tampering affecting an experiment. (Motion detectors can also fill this role.)

As well as cameras that capture the visible part of the light spectrum, there are cameras that operate in both infrared and ultraviolet frequencies. Infrared cameras are particularly useful when working in darkness as they provide clear monochrome video pictures without disturbing the vigil.

GHOST-HUNTING GADGETS

An undated photograph of Harry Price's ghost-hunting kit, comprising Reflex and cine cameras, tools for sealing doors and windows, apparatus for secret electrical controls, steel tape, drawing instruments, torch, and a bottle of mercury.

Always make sure you back up your digital pictures carefully. Never use software to enhance the original photograph, only ever work on copies—if you change the original you can never prove your anomaly is genuine, no matter how good it looks. Unfortunately, not all anomalies caught on camera are paranormal (see page 149).

Environmental monitoring

There is a wide variety of monitoring equipment, such as a simple thermometer, used to measure cold spots, a barometer measuring atmospheric pressure, a hygrometer to measure humidity, an anemometer for wind speed, and a carbon monoxide monitor to ensure those weird, giddy feelings aren't caused by a build-up of this potentially lethal gas.

Some investigators link a variety of environmental monitors to a computer system that automatically measures and logs readings throughout the vigil.

Sound-recording equipment

There are many easily available devices that record sound and they can be very valuable in gathering evidence of a haunting.

When ghostly footsteps have been reported in a certain part of the site, getting a recording is an obvious first response. Recordings of doors creaking open on their own, or banging shut, may be stone-tape-type events (see page 63) and belong to a different time period—in which case none of the present-day doors will make those particular sounds. That is something that it's well worth checking out.

Recordings during vigils of an investigator calling out and apparently being answered by a ghost making a noise, such as a tapping sound or a bang, are frequently seen on TV reality shows. They certainly make excellent viewing, particularly when the investigators are in a state of high excitement, and their faces and reactions are caught on camera.

RARE EVENTS

As anyone who has been on a vigil in an old and creaky house knows, if you ask questions often enough, an answering knock will eventually coincide with one of your questions. TV shows can be very selective in what they broadcast, just as we can be very selective about what we remember—a single prompt "answer" may be remembered clearly for years, while an entire evening without replies is soon forgotten. But that could just go to show how hard it is for spirits to communicate, how rare these real events are, how much effort we need to make to break through the veil between the worlds.

The "maybe" option

From the perspective of our digital society, familiar as we are with the on/off binary option, "yes" or "no" answers may seem routine, but it may be inappropriate to force ghosts to share our hazardous social trend of polarizing opinions. To many ghosts of a bygone age, introducing a "maybe" option would be perfectly natural, and infinitely more accommodating.

As ever, to achieve the best-quality evidence, try to use the best-quality equipment, but even

EMF Meters

 Many ghost-hunting TV shows feature electro-magnetic field (EMF) meters and frequently claim to detect a spike in levels during a phase of supposedly paranormal activity. Such spikes are usually treated as if they are scientific evidence for a paranormal event.

Unfortunately for ghost-hunters, most commercially available EMF meters are designed for electricians checking domestic and industrial wiring and appliances and this specialized purpose does not require the sort of detailed information that might be of value to a dedicated paranormal researcher. EMF meters are so common in ghost investigations that it is worth getting to know them and the way they behave. But you should do this in a non-haunted environment,

While there are many mundane reasons why an EMF meter might show a spike of activity, theories as to why ghosts might produce them tend to be less clear. One possible use is to detect EIFs (Experience-Inducing Fields), but EMF meters tend to be too crude to differentiate these fields from others.

There is a bewildering array of meters available and detailed information on which might suit your needs can be difficult to obtain from unbiased sources.

inexpensive kit is useful. Wireless microphones are usually best avoided as they are prone to pick up radio transmissions, but even the more ordinary types of microphone can pick up electromagnetic interference from, for example, mobile phones.

Using a spirit level

How do you measure a ghost? With a spirit level! The human body is astonishingly sensitive to the environment and our sense of balance (the vestibular system) is particularly finely tuned. The floors in many old buildings slope slightly and if the slant is noticeable, we can consciously compensate. But if the slope is just too slight to notice (or we are distracted by, say, a tense and dimly lit vigil), then walking across it can cause an imbalance between the different parts of our mind and body. This imbalance can make us feel unsettled, giddy, or even nauseous. Sensations such as these, experienced when we are looking for unusual phenomena, can all too easily be attributed to a spirit presence manifesting in that particular room. An ordinary spirit level can provide a measurable assessment of this easily overlooked factor.

The Evil that Lurks

 THE DARK ENTRY
Canterbury Cathedral, Kent, UK, is often called the "home of Christianity" in England and on its north side is an ancient, arched portal known as the Dark Entry. This connects to the cloisters through a vaulted passage that amplifies every sound into a mass of eerie echoes. Here, late on Friday nights after the cathedral is safely closed to tourists, walks the ghostly figure of tragic Nell Cook.

THE JEALOUS LOVER
Nell (also known as Ellen Bean) perished in the early decades of the 16th century, in an agony brought about by her extreme love for an unworthy man. He was a canon of the cathedral who lived by the Dark Entry and she was his cook. When the canon brought his lover into his house, under the guise that he was merely looking after his "niece," Nell was distraught. She secretly watched them and her love seethed and gradually boiled away, making her feel extremely jealous. Her heart hardened, her sweet nature soured, and she put poison in the pie the canon and his lover ate for dinner.

The canon and his "niece" were found dead, their bodies blackened by the poison, and they were buried hastily, but very discretely, in the cathedral's nave. Nell disappeared, but for three days and three nights, the area around the Dark Entry was haunted by moans, howls, and shrieks. Although the clergy exchanged looks that spoke volumes, none talked openly of the terrible sounds that seemed to come from the ground itself. And then all became still.

GRUESOME DISCOVERY
A century went by and a large flagstone by the Dark Entry became loose. Three masons were asked to fix it and when they raised the granite slab they discovered Nell's skeleton, her bony fingers still clutching a crust of the poisonous pie. But that wasn't the worst of it, for the legend relates how the three burly masons died shortly afterward as did many others who had seen the ghost of poor Nell Cook. For her spirit had been released from the tomb, which was sealed by the clergy, who kept the secret until it was forgotten, all those long, dark years ago. Nell Cook's ghost still haunts the Dark Entry, and to see her is said to be an omen of death.

This story may be found in serious books devoted to ghosts and is naturally widespread on the Internet. But few people realize it was written by the Reverend Richard Harris Barham, who published a wide variety of witty and humorous stories and poems, often as deliberate parodies of various types of medieval folklore. He was born in Canterbury in 1788, and the poem "Nell Cook" appears in *The Ingoldsby Legends* (written under the pen name of Thomas Ingoldsby), which is a collection of his writings published in magazines during the 1830s and 1840s. Many of these legends are tall tales involving caricatures of devils, witches, and ghosts—all behaving badly.

To all intents and purposes these poems appear to be supernatural fables, deftly written yet always tongue-in-cheek. To many readers, the story of Nell is obviously a complete fabrication composed, like Frankenstein's monster, of elements drawn from many sources and assembled in the laboratory of the author's imagination. Barham simply worked his magic and brought the phantasmagoria to life in a single, new creation.

NELL COOK—FACT OR FICTION?
In his *Memoir of Reverend Richard Harris Barham*, introducing an edition of *The Ingoldsby Legends*, Richard Harris Dalton Barham (a close relative) declares Nell to be a true Kentish legend. And another author states that the poem was based on an ancient Canterbury legend. But these are both secondary sources, commenting on the poem written by Reverend Barham. Neither quotes any earlier source. So the suspicion remains that they had fallen into the trap of trusting the poet who, in the preface to his 1842 edition, blithely assures his reader that this narrative, like all his other offerings, is true. The question is, would you mount a vigil at this site without checking the story further?

John Hippisley, author of *Haunted Canterbury* (2009) and award-winner for his Canterbury

Ghost Tour has considered the origin of the ghost of the Dark Entry. Even with his extensive local knowledge, John was unable to confirm that Barham hadn't invented this ghost story for his rhyme.

Perhaps an investigation, properly directed, might shed new light on the story. But one thing is certain: to hold a vigil without being aware of the controversy would leave you wide open to public ridicule. Imagine being accused of believing a nonsense poem!

PLAINSONG
In passing, we may note there are several other well-known ghost stories associated with Canterbury Cathedral, so the site would be worthy of investigating—if anyone could obtain permission. One of these is the sound of plainsong, an early form of devotional singing unaccompanied by instruments. It was actually heard in the vicinity of the Dark Entry, emanating from the securely locked and empty cathedral crypt. Another is the ghost of archbishop Simon Sudbury, murdered in 1381, who is said to roam the Cathedral as a pale figure with a long, gray, flowing beard. A ghostly monk, lost in perpetual contemplation, has also been seen in the cloisters.

On the Day of the Vigil

Make sure you are happy with the idea of the vigil. If you are feeling ill at ease with the prospect, even if you're not sure why, you should cancel. You are bound to be excited and nervous, but if you have a bad feeling about the venture, you should trust your intuition and not go.

Steadying the nerves

There is a moment at the start of every single investigation when you can either walk away or commit yourself. This is the time to take a deep breath, leave behind daily worries, and become a paranormal professional. In a team, this pause can be a group bonding exercise. Some groups say a prayer together; others use a grounding exercise (see pages 130–1).

You may also wish to energize an auric shield or armor—an envelope of light that surrounds the entire body. This may be filled from a perpetual source of golden light that emanates just above the head. Or you may prefer the shape of a sphere, which effortlessly penetrates the ground beneath. In either instance, you can reinforce it during the vigil whenever you feel threatened or ill at ease, and your co-workers can help with this, visualizing your collective defences.

Making a photographic survey

A photographic survey should precede every vigil as it provides a baseline record of the premises. It can give invaluable evidence in a wide variety of

situations, particularly where small items, such as ornaments or books, or even furniture are said to have been moved by supernatural forces. Regardless of whether you take a series of stills or use a video camera, be methodical. Include the vigil location, the exterior of the site, and perhaps the approach to it. It isn't always easy to tell what may become significant, so it's best to take more pictures than you think you need.

Be Prepared

In particular, pay attention to...

→ *Routine—follow routine, but emphasize peace and enjoyment.*

→ *Tomorrow—keep the day after the vigil clear, to rest, debrief, and recover.*

→ *Food and drink—eat well, with plenty of carbohydrates and don't drink alcohol for 24 hours before the vigil.*

→ *Bathing—soothe away stress from the past and tension about the future.*

→ *Clothes—fresh, warm, natural fibers are recommended.*

→ *Scent—avoid wearing perfumed cosmetics (which may mask ghostly odors.)*

→ *Jewelry—hidden beneath garments is fine, but bright rings cause light anomalies.*

Anna and the Rope Necklace

In 2009 I investigated Arnos Manor Hotel, Bristol, UK, and invited psychic artist Stephen Cox to visit and see what spirits he might find. He produced several fascinating sketches of resident ghosts. The first of these was drawn in the chapel (the hotel was previously used as a convent), where he drew a portrait of a young woman called Anna. She had a loose rope around her neck.

Stephen hadn't visited the site before and didn't notice the design on the carpet—which featured exactly the same twisted loop. He'd drawn the rope as a symbol of Anna's link to the site, a bond of loyalty and commitment (it might also have religious connotations if she was, as suspected, becoming a nun herself.)

But the questions remain: did the motif on the carpet subconsciously inspire him to incorporate it into the picture (after all, there are many ways to depict such a link), or did the carpet buyer select that pattern because it felt "right," guided by Anna's strong personal ties to the place? The striking similarity between Anna's symbol and the carpet certainly suggests something more than coincidence may be at work.

Above: *Psychic artist Stephen Cox drawing Anna.*

Far left: *The drawing of Anna wearing her unusual rope necklace.*

Left: *Detail of the carpet showing the same twisted "rope" design.*

Getting Grounded

 Anyone preparing to enter a haunted environment, or trying to live in one, can take a range of measures to strengthen themselves. One of the most powerful of these is to cultivate a frame of mind that is stable and in touch with the positive aspects of our physical life on Earth.

Being "grounded" can mean having your liberty curtailed as a punishment dealt out by parents, to prevent something bad from happening (again). But no such negative connotations should be inferred when talking about the realm of ghosts. However, there is a similarity because in both instances a thoughtless, potentially dangerous, act is avoided.

It is easy for us to let enthusiasm carry us away, and we may even lose our grip on reality for a while. It's only natural. But when we're deliberately putting ourselves in a certain amount of peril, by confronting our fear of the unknown, for example, it's sensible to minimize risks. And in any case, when the imagination runs away from us we're not going to collect very good evidence from our experience. Getting grounded improves our chances of a good-quality paranormal investigation, and reduces the risk of feeling unwell afterward.

To ground yourself, you might choose a sunny day and find an old tree to sit comfortably beneath. Holding or wearing a talismanic pentagram (see page 176) during this meditation can energize it.

1. Sit on the ground with your back to the tree, arms by your sides. Stretch out your legs, keeping them together.

2. Imagine a soft, white radiance above your head in the tree's canopy.

3. As you breathe in, a light ray flows down to your crown, shining through into your mind. Stress, anxiety, and other negative energies stick in this light like autumn leaves landing on a woodland stream.

4. These rays are carried down as you breathe out, as the light flows down through your trunk and arms, along your legs and out of your body through your feet. It flows into the Earth, taking all the debris and darkness with it, downward, where it is recycled and made wholesome. It is food for the tree and the energy flows up through the tree's roots, through its trunk and into the canopy, glowing softly with pure life that you breathe in.

5. When you feel thoroughly cleansed and refreshed, imagine the light ray shrinking as it ceases to flow into you. It ceases to flow out, leaving you full of pure, gentle, white light. Breathe the natural air.

Trees can energize and ground us.

6. Get up and stand relaxed, with your feet comfortably apart.

7. Raise your arms up at your sides and stretch. Your body is the pentagram, limbs, heart, and head, like the tree behind you. Roots, trunk, and canopy, you are the human pentagram—grounded but free.

8. Just as you finish stretching and are about to relax and walk away, pause for a moment. Feel aware of the firmness of your body and the sheer vitality of our life force—and share this joyous feeling with the pentagram, as if it is a friend. Such sharing will not diminish your experience, but it will empower the talisman,

which can then remind you and replenish your energy whenever you need it.

This meditation can be very powerful, with your feet feeling as though they are embedded solidly in the Earth, spreading deep into the ground, like the tree's roots.

But unlike the tree, which is rooted to the spot, you are free to move. With that freedom comes responsibility, and you should care not only for that tree, whose strength nurtured your meditation, but for the whole family tree you share with all life on Earth.

Ghost-Hunting Experiments

TRY DIFFERENT APPROACHES

You can try out a wide range of activities and experiments at most investigation sites, but use your common sense and intuition to guide you. If there is any doubt that a particular experiment is suitable, it should be abandoned.

Making a record

It is rarely easy to write down a record of what you are doing at the same time as doing it, so members of a group should take it in turns to take the lead and to keep the log. On a lone vigil, a video camera or sound recorder can do the same important job of documenting events. The best experiment to try at a haunted site is to use the imagination to devise an experiment tailored to the site. This is not always fruitful, but is always worth trying.

Take photographs, make sketches

It is always worth using a camera to see if it captures anything. If you are using flash with other people around, remember to say "flash" clearly a second or two before you take the shot. This allows people to close their eyes and not be blinded by the light, losing their night vision, which usually takes several minutes to recover. Sit quietly and see what images, thoughts, and impressions come to mind. Sketch these on suitable blank paper, in pencil or using colored pastels. Psychic art is always revealing, even if you think you can't draw.

Try psychometry

Touch the walls to sense whether there are any impressions left there. Try other parts of the fabric of the building, such as old fireplaces, timber beams, and doorways.

Call out

Do not feel obliged to try calling out as, despite being a mainstay of TV reality ghost hunts, it is actually an advanced technique and should only be attempted when you are feeling fully grounded and safe. Talk to spirits respectfully, stressing that you mean them no harm, and invite good spirits with the same kind intentions to respond. Ask them to reveal themselves in a friendly fashion, visibly or through noises.

At the end of any such session it is important to thank the spirits for attending, tell them that the meeting is at an end, and bid them goodbye.

SEATED GHOST →

This atmospheric photograph shows a person, perhaps a "ghost," sitting in an abandoned house in California, USA. Because photographs such as this are easy to fake, many serious investigators habitually ignore them.

Using trigger objects

Another popular experiment conducted during vigils is the positioning and monitoring of trigger objects. These are placed in haunting hot spots in the hope that they will be moved by paranormal activity. The items should be selected with some care, so as to be relevant to the haunting. For example, if the ghost is a child, you can use toys. As well as creating a connection with the ghost, who may handle them out of familiarity, these items may build a bridge of trust with the spirit.

When relevant objects are unavailable, coins are often used. You can select coins of the same date or period as the origin of the haunting. If you do not know a date for the ghost, then a range of dates should be used (if only one coin moves, then perhaps the date on that coin could provide a valuable clue). You can place small objects on a sheet of paper or card and carefully draw around them. This part of the site should then be cordoned off to prevent accidental displacement. Sprinkling objects with a powder, such as flour, can also show whether they have been moved.

Securing the site

Ideally, the site should be made inaccessible by locking the door, and surveillance equipment, such as video cameras, employed to catch the moment of movement. If you can't get hold of a video camera, use a sound recorder to catch, for example, the sound of an electrical appliance switching on and off, which could set up vibrations powerful enough to move the object. As always, before you interpret physical evidence

AUTOMATIC WRITING

Irish medium and author of more than 20 books, Geraldine Cummins (1890–1969) specialized in automatic writing—which she called "transmitted" writing—over which she exercised no conscious control or censorship.

Automatic Writing

This is different from psychic art, in which we simply draw what we intuit. Automatic writing is a form of spirit possession.

The experimenter holds a pen or pencil over a blank sheet of paper, as if they were about to draw or write something, but instead of doing so they invite a spirit to use their hand and guide what is written or drawn. Although very simple to set up, this technique is potentially one of the most dangerous of all seance experiments because the sitter may lack the expertise to ensure their personal safety. In particular, difficulties may arise because the sitter cannot effectively screen the spirits and allow only benign spirits access to their body. And, once in control of the sitter's hand, the spirit may be reluctant to depart in peace.

Given the potential for such problems, although this is a technique that can produce very interesting results, it is not recommended for any but the most experienced and capable of mediums.

as being paranormal, you should investigate all possible normal explanations. To investigate the movement of trigger objects, it is usually helpful to return to the scene as soon as you can and replicate as many of the conditions as possible. It is, for example, best to repeat the experiment at the same time of day or night, and monitor the object with all the equipment at your disposal. This will help you to gather all the data you can if the movement recurs.

Electronic Voice Phenomena

Recording sound in the hope of capturing Electronic Voice Phenomena (EVP) is a controversial but popular technique used by many paranormal investigators. EVP is recorded sound that has an apparently paranormal source. A common example is a whispered word or phrase that nobody has heard spoken, perhaps as an answer to someone calling out in a vigil.

A common problem with EVP recordings is if the microphone was not set securely on a non-vibrating surface and the recording is marred, or even drowned out, by the rustling sounds of clothing or footsteps while being carried around, or simply by being handled. Another problem with EVP is that many microphones are strongly directional. This means they not only fail properly to pick up sounds that come from behind them, but the noises directly in front of them are recorded at a higher volume than expected. This

"THE DEVIL"

This ghostly apparition, digitally altered by the photographer, is supposed to represent the Devil. If, as some suppose, the Devil is author of lies, illusions, and time-wasting trickery, then many allegedly paranormal photographs are diabolical self-portraits!

Unless we learn about our ghost-hunting technology, we will be fooled by it. If we fail to study how our own senses and mind work, our pursuit of understanding will lead us around in circles.

can explain why the playback might baffle investigators who didn't remember hearing anything that loud.

To make matters worse, many recorders automatically adjust their sensitivity to keep the playback at a fairly even volume—this is the auto-gain circuit, and often it cannot be turned off. During quiet periods, these recorders amplify all incoming signals. When the recording is played back, what was actually very quiet sounds so loud that nobody could have failed to hear it— giving the impression that the sound had a paranormal origin. It isn't paranormal, it's just a situation outside everyday experience.

Get to know your equipment

It is impossible to over-emphasize the importance of becoming familiar with your equipment. If you are fooled by it and make mistaken claims about evidence of paranormal activity, you not only embarrass yourself professionally, but help to bring the entire community of dedicated researchers into disrepute.

The safest way to analyze anomalous findings is to share them with other reputable groups. They may have come across something similar and can offer a mundane explanation. On the other hand, if you have captured something special, they will be able to advise you on the best way to publicize findings. It may seem disappointing at the time, but even if a seemingly exciting discovery turns out to have a natural explanation, a valuable lesson will have been learned.

Planchette

 The planchette device is used to draw pictures or write messages. The experimenters each place a finger on the small board, which is mounted on bearings and carries a pen. More versatile than the Ouija board, and arguably less dangerous than automatic writing, it nevertheless has the same practical and ethical difficulties as the Oujia board (see pages 138–9).

The Ouija Board

 The Ouija board was patented in 1890 and it evolved from a variety of "talking boards" that 19th-century mediums used in seances to assist spirits to communicate by spelling out messages. In its simplest form, the talking board consists of the letters of the alphabet and numerals, arranged in a circle. Additional options such as "yes," "no," and "goodbye" are often used. In the center is an object, such as a tablet on bearings (a "planchette"—see page 137), large enough for several people to place a finger on. This slides around, spelling out messages. In many home-made versions, this pointer is an upturned glass.

The sitting is usually held by candlelight, which helps provide atmosphere, and the sitters each place an index finger on the planchette. The leader will call out to the spirit world for someone to communicate through them, by moving the pointer. The phrase "Is there anyone there?" is such a cliché that it is seldom used these days, since chuckling tends to defuse any spooky atmosphere.

DIFFICULTIES WITH OUIJA

The use of the Ouija board is often frowned upon by mediums as being inherently unsafe, and some are even as definite as, say, fundamentalist Christians in forbidding its use. Part of the problem is that the Ouija is often regarded as an entry-level tool; something that anyone can use. Because the beginner has no idea how to protect him- or herself there is, some mediums say, a real danger that when they call out and invite spirits to communicate, they may attract malevolent ghosts, or even more dangerous spirits masquerading as ghosts. Once summoned in this way, it may be difficult to persuade evil spirits to leave.

The rational explanation for how Ouija boards seem to work is based on our body's complex dynamic feedback system that constantly monitors and controls our actions. This involuntary, or unconscious, behavior is known as "ideomotor" action, and underlies other paranormal phenomena such as automatic writing and dowsing.

Extending an arm exerts a constant muscular strain that is difficult to maintain. We instinctively allow our muscles to fluctuate slightly, tightening and loosening them almost imperceptibly. These random contractions and extensions from each of the participants sometimes cancel each other out, but other times aggregate into a force strong enough to move the pointer. Those who support Ouija say that this physical explanation does not discredit the practice, it merely describes the way spirits use our willingness to surrender our involuntary muscular movements. The spirits are able to influence us in subtle ways that, cumulatively, make a big difference.

A Ouija board in action.

Once the inertia of the pointer is overcome, its apparently random direction adds an additional difficulty for us as we try to keep our finger on it. Our efforts to keep up with its movements simply add force to the movement itself.

We may have explained why the planchette moves, but if the sceptics are right and the movements are random, surely the message would be meaningless too. In many cases the message is disturbingly meaningful. Sometimes the message spells out D E A T H and moves toward one of the sitters in an ominous indication of the intended victim.

Discounting conscious trickery, there are numerous psychological factors, such as primed expectation, peer pressure, and even just a knowledge of spelling and grammar, that all contribute to ideomotor action and influence the journey of the pointer from letter to letter and word to word. Only if the message is verifiable objectively, from a source that none of the sitters could have known, can it be said to have a paranormal origin.

Because of the persuasive, mundane explanation for the moving pointer and the difficulty in assessing the results, the value of using tools such as the Ouija board is severely limited. Coupled with the ongoing controversy over whether the technique is psychologically or spiritually safe, the best advice is probably simply not to take it seriously.

Top Ten Ghost-Hunters

This is a list of the top ten most well-known ghost-hunters, both past and present.

→ **Zak Bagans** *(born 1977, Las Vegas, USA) is the lead investigator in the TV series* Ghost Adventures. *His provocative style of summoning spirits to produce phenomena makes popular entertainment, but has yet to find credibility with many mediums or serious researchers.*

→ **Yvette Fielding** *(born 1968, Stockport, UK) became the public face of ghost-hunting in the early 21st century. Her empathy projected the emotional rollercoaster of ghost-hunting into viewers' homes, with shows such as* Most Haunted.

→ **Jason Hawes** *(born 1971, New York, USA) and Grant Wilson (born 1974, Rhode Island, USA) are founders of The Atlantic Paranormal Society (TAPS), and star in the TV series* Ghost Hunters. *Their down-to-earth approach is evidence-based and seeks natural explanations for phenomena before suspecting paranormal activity is involved.*

→ **Harry Houdini** *(1874–1926, born in Budapest, Hungary) was a sceptic who used his abilities as a stage magician to expose fraudulent practices among mediums, often discovering tricks that academics had never dreamed of. For a decade after his death his widow conducted seances, but he failed to make contact.*

→ **Ciarán O'Keeffe** *(born 1971, Norwich, UK) is a parapsychologist with a particular interest in assessing evidence of ghostly phenomena. He has embraced media interest in the paranormal, and joined the* Most Haunted *team in 2004, where his calm and cautious approach proved to be a valuable foil to the antics of other members.*

→ **Harry Price** *(1881–1948, born in London, UK) exposed numerous fraudulent mediums, but became convinced that some were genuine. He used a wide range of equipment to investigate hauntings, most famously the Borley Rectory poltergeist, which he studied for 16 years.*

→ **James Randi** *(born 1928, Toronto, Canada) is well-known as a stage magician, but best known as a debunker of false claims of paranormal ability. His 1964 offer of $1,000 cash reward for proof of psychic, supernatural, or paranormal ability remains unclaimed, even though the reward has now risen to $1 million.*

→ **Troy Taylor** *(born 1966, Decatur, USA) is the author of around fifty ghost books. He founded the American Ghost Society, and the Haunted Museum, Illinois, which houses exhibits relating to spiritualism and paranormal investigation.*

→ **Peter Underwood** *(born 1923, Letchworth, UK) is one of the most prolific writers about ghosts, with around 50 books detailing the full range of British hauntings. Among his many credits, he is life president of the Ghost Club Society, and patron of PSI (Paranormal Site Investigators).*

→ **Dave Wood** *(born 1981, Isle of Skye, UK) is a founding member of PSI. The group's primary aims are to educate people about anomalous experiences and conduct scientific research.*

↑

HARRY PRICE, GHOST-HUNTER

This photograph shows Harry Price ghost-watching from a summer house, in 1945. One of the first valuable skills an investigator acquires is passive alertness: hours may pass without incident, yet split-second reactions are required when something does happen.

VERIFYING FINDINGS

If you do contact someone to verify your findings, you need to be careful how you approach them. It's rather like talking to someone about a movie you've seen—if they haven't seen it you can inadvertently spoil their enjoyment by telling them too much about the plot. If you tell a paranormal researcher what you think the voice is saying, they will find it almost impossible to hear anything else. So you should just explain where the recording was taken, to give them the context, but not give the game away by telling them what you think it actually says.

The problem is the same as pareidolia (see page 144). If you are shown a piece of burnt toast and are told the pattern looks like a soul in torment and you see the image, you'll probably never see the ordinary piece of toast, ever again. It will always have the soul superimposed on it. We're always trying to find order in chaos and it's much easier for us to learn something than to unlearn it.

Pareidolia is also responsible for much of what we hear in EVP recordings (see page 135). Although the recording might be of wind whistling through a draughty window, you might hear it say "Hello" or "Henry," or even "Heaven help you." Whatever recordings you make, it is vital you archive them safely. If you undertake any editing or other enhancement or manipulation (including converting it to a different digital file format) you must make sure you work on a copy and keep the original unaltered. This is the only way to ensure an independent analyst can check and confirm your findings.

After the Vigil

FALSE POSITIVES

One of the biggest problems in conducting paranormal research in the field rather than the laboratory is the difficulty of avoiding false positives. These are phenomena reported as paranormal, but which actually have a normal origin. Training ourselves to recognize the range of natural but unusual phenomena is a significant challenge. At three o'clock in the morning, with tension running high in a spooky old house, it can be very hard not to get jittery. Being aware of a theory is not the same as experiencing the real thing. But when it comes to analyzing the results of the vigil, the following factors should be helpful in identifying and discounting many false-positive incidents.

Primed expectations

Powerful psychological factors make us inclined to see what we expect to see. We each carry around a mental map of what we think the world is like. We all know that mind-boggling moment of mental readjustment when we encounter something very unusual—"I couldn't believe my eyes!" Even if the experience isn't actually paranormal, the strikingly unexpected causes a mental shock, throwing the mind into momentary confusion while we struggle to look for a suitable explanation. People frequently opt to believe in a religious or other paranormal explanation for what is actually perfectly normal and natural— just very unusual.

Nun-tinted spectacles

There are two main drawbacks to knowing all about a site before you visit. Firstly, if for example you know a haunted building had been a convent, thoughts are bound to be fired up with ideas about nuns, religious devotion, and the social interactions of a closed community.

As soon as you walk through the door, you can't help but see the site through nun-tinted spectacles, and anything you experience will be seen against the backdrop of convent life. If you see a shadowy shape from the corner of your eye, the first thing you'd think of is a nun in a habit, or a shady monk. Expectations mold perceptions.

The second problem is that, even if you encounter a fully materialized nun, a sceptic will discount the experience because he or she will argue it was simply the imagination playing tricks.

SUCCESSFUL GHOST-HUNTER

A successful ghost-hunter, seen in action during the 1950s, watches an apparition apparently walk through a solid wall. Such clear empirical evidence with (presumably) multiple witnesses, is frequently found in fiction, but is, in fact, something of a holy grail for researchers.

Even if you have not been told the details of the site's history, you might still have accidentally heard about it before, possibly years earlier. The visit could jog the memory, so that the mind subconsciously conjures up a spectral nun to step out of nowhere with a greeting from the dim and distant past. So, while thorough historical research can prevent investigating a story that is really a waste of time, it can also prevent us from investigating properly. In a team it may make sense to take it in turns, so that sometimes you can arrive at the vigil site knowing absolutely nothing about what you might find.

Haunted, the movie
However, sometimes choosing to know nothing can be a perilous decision. In the scary movie *Haunted* (1995), a professor and psychologist answers an old housekeeper's pleas for help with the ghosts that torment her in the large, secluded old house she tends. He arrives to find several other people are staying—younger members of the family that owns it. The professor (Aidan Quinn) is seduced by the amoral young woman,

We are all blinkered by our expectations. If we cannot see any truth in that, we are blind indeed. Fortunately, such spiritual or psychological darkness is rarely permanent.

BELMEZ HAUNTED HOUSE

A photograph dated 4 February 1972 shows the first face displayed on Maria Gomez's kitchen floor in Andalusia. The mystery of the "Belmez's faces" began on 23 August 1971, when strange marks started appearing in her home.

played by Kate Beckinsale, and although he finds no evidence of a haunting, he decides to stay a little longer. Of course, his beguiling hostess and her two brothers are, in fact, the ghosts, and he finds it very difficult indeed to leave.

PAREIDOLIA
The mind is vigilant in searching for patterns in the environment. This is how we learn new things and avoid dangerous situations. But in its efforts to show us all the patterns it can possibly find, it becomes over-zealous and sometimes the result is that we see a pattern that really isn't there.

Seeing things
The "man in the Moon" is one of the best-known examples of seeing something that isn't really there. And once we've seen the smiling face of the Galle crater on Mars, it is hard to see anything but a smiley. We don't need Rorschach inkblot cards to start seeing examples of pareidolia. We can find animals in clouds, saints in burnt toast, a ghost in a patch of moonlight, and meaning in chaos wherever we happen to look.

As a triumph of imagination over reality, we are dealing with hallucinations, but once we learn to recognize them for what they are, their tyranny loses much of its power over us. However, in a vigil extending into the small hours of the morning, when our brain is normally asleep, it can easily populate the darkness with dreamlike visions. And, just like a dream, they can seem very real—at the time.

SHADOWS IN THE DARK

A great many ghost sightings are of moving shadows glimpsed from the corner of an eye. These are usually of a shapeless figure that seems to be enveloped in some sort of dark, head-to-toe cloak—a monk wearing a hooded habit might be a typical description in Europe. In the USA, which lacks the deeply engrained memory of medieval monasticism, they may be perceived as dark, demonic figures, or furtive aliens.

This sort of experience is easily explained as a trick of our peripheral vision. At the eye's periphery, the receptor cells are mostly rod-shaped and only register the suble shades of light and dark. These cells are our evolutionary adaptation for evading predators and they are especially quick to detect movement, particularly at night.

> All the great investigators, whether sceptics or believers, have one thing in common, and it's something we can all do. They simply decided to find out for themselves.

Noticing things

In times or places of heightened awareness, such as a haunting situation when the senses are straining to notice anything unusual, as attention shifts you may seem to notice things you had overlooked before. This creates an impression of something that is new, something that has changed something that has moved.

Of course, when you actually see one of these things, it can be a powerfully moving experience, literally—people often jump and many gasp or shriek. For a split second the primal instinct of fight-or-flight is triggered by what we perceive to be an attack by a terrifying entity. It is only later, when we realize that no lurking darkness actually leaped out at us, that we recognize the experience for what it almost certainly was—a trick of the eye.

A HOODED MONK?

The mind can work overtime when the person sees quite normal things, and it is no wonder that ghosts have been poetically called "shades"—shadows. This "ghostly" figure is a photograph of a shadow on a graveyard gate.

Infrasound

 Just as our eyes can only see a part of the spectrum of light, so our ears can only hear some of the sounds that surround us, typically between 20 and 20,000 vibrations per second (Hz). Infrasound is sound that is too low in pitch for us to hear (below 20 Hz.) If it is loud enough, we can feel it.

A researcher had the pleasure of a good night's sleep in the most haunted room at the Royal Castle Hotel, Dartmouth, UK, and awoke in a cosy four-poster bed around dawn with a very peculiar sensation. It was as if the whole room was banging like a drum—but the drum was somehow inside his body. The rhythmic vibration was inaudible but powerful. A baby in the womb must feel its mother's heartbeat this way.

The experience arose from the architecture of the 17th-century building. The guest rooms were on several floors around a central atrium with wooden stairs and walkways. When the staff hurried along a particular section of ancient woodwork, their footfalls resonated in the haunted room at an infrasound frequency. There are many other sources of infrasound, including the rumble of road traffic, trains, and drills, as well as the chaotic noise of running water, wind, storms, and earthquakes. Some ordinary household appliances, such as fans and refrigerators, can also emit infrasound.

NEW-HOUSE SYNDROME

When several powerful factors combine they can produce a catalog of reported phenomena. Sometimes, though, a single, simple explanation can be found—"new-house syndrome."

When you first move into a new environment you notice everything about it. You observe every little sound, such as central heating, the bangs and thuds of thermal expansion and contraction, the way floorboards creak when someone walks across them, the way noise coming out of a neighbor's window echoes off a brick wall and sounds strangely loud in a particular bedroom. You notice all the little draughts that cause cold spots, all the flashes from passing traffic that reflect sunlight into the rooms, all the faint smells that rise from the garden or that damp patch you haven't yet discovered under the bath. After a while, you learn to recognize which recurring events are merely insignificant distractions. You get used to them and become desensitized. Eventually you ignore them. But what if somebody tells you the house is haunted? You begin to notice all the thousands of little events all over again. The house seems to come alive. Surely it wasn't like that before! But it was; you had just stopped noticing. And if you visit a place you've been told is haunted, you will notice everything because you are on the lookout for phenomena. But you will have no way of telling which are normal events and which are related to the haunting. This is one reason why every site benefits from several visits during a proper, longitudinal investigation.

Thermal expansion and contraction

Physics tells us that when most objects warm up they expand and when they cool they contract. In a house with wooden joists, the joint where two pieces of timber touch can creak loudly as one moves against the other. Such noises may range from dull thuds or sharp cracks to an inaudible infrasound that may be felt rather than heard. The effect of central heating can also contribute to this, and hot water flowing through pipes may suddenly cause them to shift slightly.

PHOTOGRAPHIC ANOMALIES

Because it is often assumed that "the photograph cannot lie," many people allow photographs to convince them of the existence of ghosts. However, photography is capable of playing many tricks on us. One of the most common is where the flash bounces off reflective surfaces, producing a bright spot. The camera has captured something strange, but not paranormal. Another example is in cold conditions when breath condenses, billowing in front of the camera, sometimes creating an ethereal, misty figure.

> By recognizing the many ways we can be mislead, we learn to avoid wasting time investigating incidents that, while unusual, are not paranormal. By concentrating our efforts on what remains unexplained, with a bit of luck, we may make a breakthrough.

Automatic cameras

In low light an automatic camera might use a combination of flash and slow shutter speed to light the scene. If the camera is hand-held, there may be camera-shake, and if there is a light source in view, it might create a jerky or swirling line. When the flash fires it captures the rest of the picture pin sharp, but there will be a weird streak of light on the picture. The photographer wouldn't have seen anything unusual while taking the picture.

Film cameras

With certain film cameras there is the possibility of creating a double exposure, superimposing two separate images on top of each other, with fabulously ghostlike results, which can look very convincing. This is usually a deliberate hoax rather than a chance occurrence.

Digital cameras

Digital images may be enhanced or completely altered using picture-editing software. Identifying such hoaxes is a specialist study in itself.

FLASH PHOTOGRAPHY ANOMALIES

A variety of photographic anomalies are most likely to manifest when flash is used.

Orbs

The most common and well known of these is the "orb," a disc of light superimposed on the background of the picture. Because they are always circular and never seen edge-on, people assume they are spherical, hence "orb."

Orbs exploded onto the paranormal scene shortly after cheap digital cameras were introduced and many people honestly believed that the emerging technology had finally captured proof of spirit activity, particularly as some of the orbs appear to have faces in them.

However, extensive tests established beyond reasonable doubt that they are caused by particles of dust floating in the air close to the camera lens. The flash unit on these cameras was positioned so that any speck of dust would be lit brightly. The brilliantly lit dust (more accurately, its highlight or most reflective part) would also be out of focus to the point that it appears as a transparent disc. The "faces" are merely random attributes in the dust, which are given human characteristics through the effect of pareidolia (see page 144.)

Insects

Other natural objects that cause orb-like anomalies include flying insects, which can be particularly impressive when they are seen in video footage, illuminated by the camera lights during nocturnal vigils.

Rain drops

Rain drops can produce strange-looking orbs—like teardrops in shape, but upside down, as if they were shooting upward into the air. The drop of rain, like the dust in an ordinary orb, is close to the lens and catches the flash. The tail effect is created when the camera is focusing on something that is actually too far away for the flash to illuminate it properly.

Unlike in normal circumstances, in which the flash switches on and then cuts off, here it switches on at full power, keeps trying to illuminate the scene, but inevitably dims as the capacitor is drained of electricity. All this time the rain drop carries on moving, and the lower it falls the less light is coming from the flash—hence the pale tail below the bright top. In a rural setting these orbs can resemble fairy sprites darting up out of the vegetation.

Armchair Ghost-Hunting

Few of us have the opportunity to join a real paranormal investigation team, but we can all enjoy vicarious thrills in the quest for evidence of life after death, just by sitting on our sofas and watching TV.

In the first decade of the 21st century, reality TV shows embraced paranormal research with unprecedented enthusiasm. The release in 2002 of *Most Haunted*, fronted by former BBC children's program presenter Yvette Fielding, captured the imagination of a public eager to believe. The show was an instant success and paved the way for a host of others, each striving to fill a gap in the market.

VICTIMS OF THEIR OWN SUCCESS

Unfortunately, some shows become victims of their own success. Ratings soar when phenomena occur, so producers often compete to capture the most entertaining phenomena. At its most extreme, such programs are not hunting ghosts— they are merely hunting ratings. And these shows cannot be said to be representative of anyone but the very worst paranormal thrill-seekers.

Extremes, though, by definition, are not the majority, and many reality shows portray people with heartfelt beliefs who are doing their honest best to help the disembodied spirits and the people they haunt.

MOST HAUNTED, TV SERIES

The team get to work in Culzean Castle, Ayreshire, Scotland, with spiritual medium Derek Acorah taking center stage. The site is associated with numerous ghosts, including a piper whose bagpipes are said to sound in celebration of marriages in the clan.

No-holds-barred Adventurers

 Ghost Adventures made its debut in 2008 and its team of three quickly established a reputation for having one of the more extreme, in-your-face approaches to paranormal investigation.

EDINBURGH VAULTS
Their aggressive tactics were particularly memorable in an Edinburgh Vaults vigil in Scotland. These 18th-century vaults had been home to some of the poorest in the city. The suffering and misery that families once endured in these lightless, airless chambers is difficult to contemplate.

The team learned from a local authority that the spirit of one particular resident—Mr. Boots—had an aversion to bright lights. Out of respect for him, the tour guide would only use living flames such as candles and oil lamps. The *Ghost Adventures* team decided to use this knowledge to coax an appearance out of the spirit. During the team's dusk-to-dawn vigil, which was their first outside of the USA, lead investigator Zak Bagans deliberately and repeatedly sought to provoke Mr. Boots by shining a bright, electric light all around the haunted room. At the same time he shouted challenges that wouldn't sound out of place in a bar-room brawl, as though he were calling an

opponent out for a fight; Mr. Boots, by all accounts, was not a nice fellow in his day, and perhaps this form of communication was one that he would readily understand. But if Zak's antics were not solely intended to make the show more exiting, the viewer is as challenged by his behavior as Mr. Boots himself. Is it acceptable, under any circumstances, to intimidate, humiliate, and bully a ghost?

In return for his efforts, Zak got a few noises, an EMF spike, and felt he was touched. All these phenomena are generally accepted on reality TV shows as evidence of the paranormal. Assuming the ghost of Mr. Boots really does haunt the Edinburgh Vaults, do we believe Zak has taught him a valuable lesson and induced him to mend his ways? From now on, will Mr. Boots be a reformed character? Or might we suppose this spirit's reaction will be different? Might Mr. Boots—or any spirit similarly insulted—experience extreme frustration and outrage, and determine to exact indiscriminate revenge?

It might make good TV to stir up a hornet's nest, and *Ghost Adventures* has run to three seasons, but while a presenter can simply walk away, the local people must live with the aftermath.

Great Ghost TV series

TV dramas have brought some great series about ghosts and hauntings into our living rooms. Here is a selection to look out for:

AFTERLIFE (2005–2006, UK)
The experiences of a middle-aged medium Alison Mundy (Lesley Sharp) are investigated by a university lecturer Robert Bridge (Andrew Lincoln). This is a scary, though not gory, drama, which met with much critical acclaim when it first came out, exploring many aspects of mediumship.

BEING HUMAN (2009–PRESENT, UK)
Annie Sawyer (Lenora Crichlow) is a modern ghost haunting the house in which she was murdered. The house is rented by John Mitchell (Aidan Turner) and George Sands (Russell Tovey), friends who happen to be a vampire and werewolf respectively. It might sound like a comedy and it has its moments, but it also explores the dark side.

GHOST WHISPERER (2005–PRESENT, USA)
Melinda Gordon (Jennifer Love Hewitt), who possesses mediumistic abilities, faces a range of constant challenges from a whole crowd of spirits who need her assistance in passing over. This can usually be achieved by redressing a wrong or completing an important task that has been left undone.

MEDIUM (2005–PRESENT, USA)
Inspired by the exploits of real-life psychic Allison DuBois (Patricia Arquette), this popular series explores a wide range of paranormal activity while concentrating on the interaction of the living with the ghosts of the dead. Allison frequently uses her abilities to assist in solving law-enforcement investigations.

RANDALL AND HOPKIRK (DECEASED) (1969–1971, 2000–2001, UK)
Two good friends run a private investigation business, until Marty Hopkirk (Kenneth Cope/ Vic Reeves) is murdered. Returning as a ghost, however, Marty carries on assisting his living partner, Jeff Randall (Mike Pratt/Bob Mortimer), in their continuing struggle to achieve justice for their clients.

SAPPHIRE AND STEEL (1979–1982, UK)
This highly popular cult series contains many references to ghosts, with Series Two devoted entirely to them, and several appearing in Series One. Sapphire (Joanna Lumley) and Steel (David McCallum) are part of a sort of supernatural special forces team, who use their paranormal abilities to defuse catastrophic situations.

SCOOBY DOO (1969–PRESENT, USA)
This remarkable team of cartoon paranormal investigators (including the eponymous dog)

A scene from Randall and Hopkirk (Deceased).

has appeared in innumerable spin-offs. Originally, all the ghosts the team investigated were fakes, but real paranormal encounters eventually became common.

SEA OF SOULS (2004–2007, UK)

Despite its evocative title, this series does not focus exclusively on ghosts and is set in a university department dealing with the paranormal in its variety of forms. The main theme concerns the head of department Douglas Monaghan (Bill Paterson), who struggles to keep his students safe as they conduct investigations into dangerous phenomena.

SUPERNATURAL (2005–PRESENT, USA)

Sam Winchester (Jared Padalecki) and Dean Winchester (Jensen Ackles) are brothers united in the quest to continue their father's work hunting and eradicating malevolent spirits and monsters, including ghosts.

TOPPER (1953–1955, USA)

Ghosts George Kerby (Robert Sterling) and his wife Marion (Anne Jeffreys) try to inject some high spirits into the life of a banker, who, following the couple's death, moves into their house. A comedy movie remake of this popular show is due to be released in 2010, starring Steve Martin.

Most Haunted

MOST TAUNTED

Most Haunted has always had its detractors and its future looked bleak in 2005 when accusations surfaced about allegedly faked communications by its star medium Derek Acorah. The allegations, published by the *Daily Mirror,* UK, which were made by the show's own independent parapsychologist Dr. Ciarán O'Keeffe, included the assertion that despite appearances to the contrary, Derek sometimes had prior knowledge of the vigil locations.

This single factor would enable Derek to research the haunted history of the venue and then produce what appeared to be a spontaneous demonstration of mediumship by making "contact" with the spirits. The presenters would confirm his contacts as matching exactly the spirits reputed to haunt the site, making his efforts appear to be impressive evidence for his psychic ability.

Viewers felt let down by the program and some complained to Ofcom, the independent organization that regulates TV broadcasts in the UK. Ofcom declared that its role was not to offer judgments about the reality, or otherwise, of paranormal activity, but it did accept it had a duty to consider these viewers' complaints.

It received complaints on several grounds, but the central issue was the viewers' perception

that fakery on the show was deceiving people into thinking that the rigged events were real. However, Ofcom sidestepped the controversy over whether or not the events were fraudulent by deciding the program was for entertainment rather than education.

They said the inclusion of celebrities in the program, the overly dramatic responses given by the presenters during incidents in the vigils, and the nature of the music and graphics were all evidence of elaborate showmanship, which would not be expected of a purely factual program. Ofcom decided the programs were not a legitimate investigation.

As such, *Most Haunted* was branded as entertainment, and could not be convicted of the complaints against it, which included serious points such as having the potential to harm vulnerable and susceptible viewers. The fact that the program-makers did not immediately seek to appeal against the decision was taken by some people to indicate an acceptance that Ofcom's decision was justified.

Most Haunted has produced numerous spin-offs such as *Most Haunted Extra, Most Haunted Live!, Most Haunted: Recurring Nightmares, Most Haunted: Midsummer Murders,* and *Most Haunted USA*, as well as *Ghost Hunting With...*, which saw Yvette team up with celebrities between 2006 and 2009. The show itself was re-branded *New Most Haunted* in 2007, and a new season aired in 2009.

As patron of the Bristol Society for Paranormal Research and Investigation, a researcher was invited to the Access all Areas arena for the *Pirates' Curse* mini-series of *Most Haunted Live,* filmed on the night of 7 May 2007. Among many memories of that event, he vividly recalls one particular incident.

One of the strengths of the *Most Haunted* team is that they keep introducing new experiments into the show. For example, their original theme of "If you're there, make a noise," had already developed into "If you're there, touch me," leading to the characteristic exclamations of surprise and wonder from the investigators that Ofcom had noted.

On the night in question, the live audience was shown some footage from the previous evening's visit to a haunted site. At one point the team of investigators split up, with individuals undertaking solo vigils in the dark. One of them offered the spirits a proposition that was obviously too good to ignore: "If you're there, touch my co-worker, who's down there on his own."

The instant shriek from the solo investigator was met by the audience with—not gasps of horror, or even a stunned silence—but howls of laughter. It was the on-stage presenter's face, though, that was so memorable. It was as if Doom had come for him in a carriage of bones drawn by headless horses. Clearly the audience's reaction was not the anticipated one. Far from being spellbound by the frightful ordeal the investigators were enduring in their lonely vigils, the audience had spontaneously and collectively decided that enough was enough and that *Most Haunted's* entertainment had degenerated into farce.

However, the on-stage presenter was admirably professional and quickly recovered his composure. He deftly drew his suddenly anarchic audience back into contact with the more serious atmosphere of the vigils. But for one moment, even its most ardent fans, who had managed to get tickets to see the live show, were not laughing along with *Most Haunted Live,* but at it.

The team's antics have continued to tend toward the extreme, as public pressure to produce exciting viewing increases with every season. One of the more alarming developments is a growing impatience on the part of the investigators, a trend seemingly led by the producer, Yvette's husband and martial artist Karl Beattie. Spirits have been subjected to verbal abuse for not revealing their presence. This technique of paranormal investigation is, sadly, not unique to *New Most Haunted*.

5
Defense Against Ghosts

Protection From the Unkown

STOPPING THINKING

Children are sometimes given reassuring advice to use for protection against their fears. One young child who became scared by the idea of ghosts was given a simple tip by his mother: "Every time you talk about them, they take a step closer." The idea that if we stop drawing them to us, ghosts will stay away, is an effective weapon against winding ourselves up or talking our companions into hysterics, but it is limited. Even if we stop talking straightaway, what if ghosts are attracted to us when we simply think about them?

Ghostbusters

In the comic movie *Ghostbusters* (1984), the team is confronted with a similar challenge. Doom is about to visit, but the team is given the power to choose the physical form that it will take. Quick-witted parapsychologist Peter Venkman (Bill Murray) suggests that they all clear their minds to prevent themselves choosing anything, so the doom cannot come. Unfortunately, Ray Stantz (Dan Aykroyd) can't help himself from thinking, so he thinks of the most harmless thing he can: marshmallows. And so their doom arrives in the surreal form of the advertizing icon of the Stay-Puft Marshmallow Man.

MEDITATION AND PRAYER

Stopping thinking takes practice, but it's a meditation worth learning. Usually, though, it is enough to halt a ghost's advance by simply diverting your mind and thinking of something else instead. Many people use a prayer, or an affirmation such as "I am protected by spirits of goodness," to compose themselves. The prayer's power may be strengthened if it is accompanied by ritual. A Christian, for instance, might make the sign of the cross, or a Wiccan might draw a pentagram in the air as a magic barrier. Learning to concentrate to the exclusion of other things is another valuable asset in our mental armory.

STOP BELIEVING

That ghost may have left us in peace for now, but some people feel the need for a more permanent solution. One way to get a trouble-free life is to stop believing in the whole idea of ghosts and rest secure in the knowledge that what doesn't exist can't harm anyone. But what if we wish to carry on entertaining the notion of ghosts and just want to be rid of one particular spirit? An exorcism might be just what we need.

GHOSTBUSTERS

The eye-catching publicity poster from this popular movie, released in 1984, showing the team in action. Their successful technological exorcisms allowed them to defend the world from an apocalyptic attack by ancient gods.

THEY'RE HERE TO SAVE THE WORLD.

BILL MURRAY DAN AYKROYD
SIGOURNEY WEAVER

GH STBUSTERS

COLUMBIA PICTURES PRESENTS

AN IVAN REITMAN FILM

A BLACK RHINO/BERNIE BRILLSTEIN PRODUCTION

"GHOSTBUSTERS"

ALSO STARRING HAROLD RAMIS AND RICK MORANIS

MUSIC BY ELMER BERNSTEIN "GHOSTBUSTERS" PERFORMED BY RAY PARKER, JR. PRODUCTION DESIGN BY JOHN DE CUIR

DIRECTOR OF PHOTOGRAPHY LASZLO KOVACS, A.S.C. VISUAL EFFECTS BY RICHARD EDLUND, A.S.C. EXECUTIVE PRODUCER BERNIE BRILLSTEIN

WRITTEN BY DAN AYKROYD AND HAROLD RAMIS PRODUCED AND DIRECTED BY IVAN REITMAN

EXORCISM AND POSSESSION

An exorcism is the attempt to get rid of evil spirits from someone who believes they are possessed or haunted. Religious rites may be used. Most people think of exorcism in terms of priests of the Roman Catholic Church performing ceremonies in Latin to banish such spirits, but this was updated at the end of the 20th century, including a presumption towards psychological illness rather than spiritual possession. The many Christian sects in the USA each have their own strategies for dealing with people suffering symptoms of possession.

The Church of England in the UK has also distanced itself from the role of exorcist, and in 1974 set up the Ministry of Deliverance, handling enquiries from those plagued with apparently supernatural problems. Every diocese has a specialist, who offers access to the Christian approach to calming anxiety. Prayers may be offered to help the victim withstand the threat; a home visit may also use prayer to invoke angels to drive away evil, and the house and occupants may also receive a blessing. In extreme cases, this process can be repeated.

CLEANSING

There are many other ways to try to cleanse a house of unwelcome spirits. Smudging, a North American Indian technique using smoke to dispel negative energy, has recently become a popular remedy for lifting the atmosphere of some suspected hauntings. But there are other methods. For instance, a house suffering from a cloying atmosphere of dismal moodiness may be cleansed by holding a bright, noisy party to drive away any drab and drowsy spirits. Feelings of freshness and uninhibited potential are the hallmarks of a successful cleansing.

Going into the light

There are many mediums willing and able to perform cleansings and most tailor their methods to the requirements of the case. A famous common denominator is the idea of "going into the light," which is usually seen as a portal through which the spirit needs to travel to find its next level of existence. However, some Earthbound spirits simply don't see the light. Perhaps unfinished business stops them feeling free to leave. Or maybe death was traumatic and left them in a state of spiritual shock, so they still need to come to terms with the fact that they are a ghost. There are as many reasons for remaining Earthbound as there are ghosts.

CONFRONTING THE UNKNOWN

The chilling movie *The Others* (2001) plays on our fear of confronting the unknown and protecting ourselves from it, with Nicole Kidman

LOST SOULS, MOVIE →

The theme of exorcism runs through this movie, made in 2000, in which John Hurt plays the part of a renegade priest and Winona Rider plays a woman struggling to be free of demonic possession.

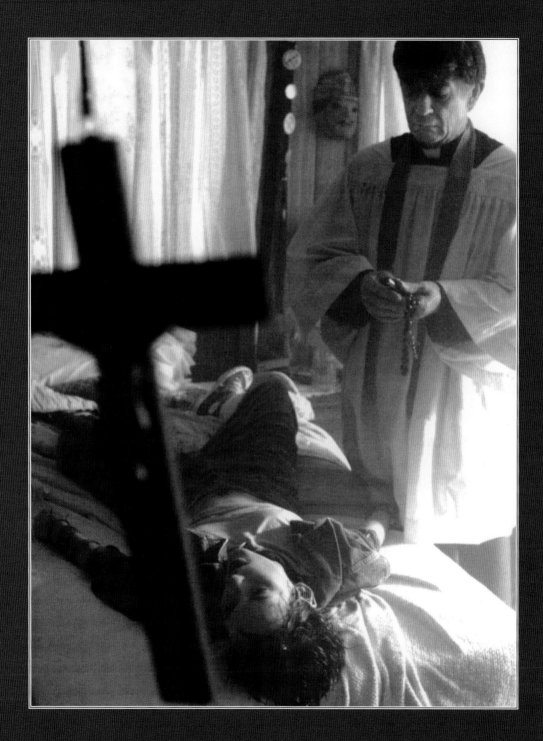

POLTERGEIST, THE MOVIE

The three *Poltergeist* movies, made during the early 1980s, were very successful. The first, from which the still above is taken, depicts a group of seemingly benign ghosts who communicate with a young girl via TV static. The movie deals with their kidnap of her and her family's efforts to get her back.

giving a magnificent performance as a young mother trying to protect her children from a terrifying supernatural ordeal. The lighter but still tensely gripping movie *Sixth Sense* (1999) stars Bruce Willis as a child psychologist. His latest patient sees dead people, especially people who don't know they're dead. Some ghosts deliberately try to avoid entering or even looking at the light. This may be because they fear punishment for past behavior, or perhaps they

Festival of Hungry Ghosts

 Starting on the night of the 14th day of the 7th month of the Chinese lunar calendar each year, the living are plagued by the souls of the starving dead. These are the souls of people who have no one to give them offerings on home altars, or bring food and drink to their graves (as during the festival of Tomb-sweeping Day, see page 48). They may also be the souls of evil-doers who have been denied sustenance as a punishment. These spirits are allowed to roam free from the Underworld once a year to find whatever nourishment they can.

People taking pity on these unfortunate spirits leave food outside their houses, often with candles or incense to attract attention. Hell Bank Money is burned to give the ghosts financial resources to take back into the Underworld, so they can feed themselves during the year ahead. These are given out of doors to avoid the danger of enticing these ravenous spirits into the home.

Many people walk in fear on this night, dreading the possibility of allowing a spirit to attach itself and settle into the household and devour the family's energy in the year ahead, draining it of good luck. The trick to escaping this fate is simple. Immediately before entering the house, an irresistible offering should be left outside. The ghost eagerly falls on it and loses track of the person, not noticing where they have gone. By giving it a little of what it craves, peace and good fortune is protected—because the ghost will not follow them into the home.

simply fear change. This dilemma of whether to go into the light or not lies at the heart of some of the most emotionally intense scenes in the first *Poltergeist* movie (1982). But unfortunately, an even deeper, diabolical trouble opens up beneath their home. It has been built on a graveyard and the family have a narrow escape when their house is sucked into a pit of damnation. We may draw a simple moral from this seminal movie: we disturb the dead at our peril.

SOUL RESCUE
Many mediums disagree with home owners who feel content to live with a ghost. Ghosts, they argue, are not like pets; they are human souls that are trapped in an alien environment—they deserve all the help they need to complete the journey that began with their death, the journey into the realms of spirit. Such views have been expressed by psychics such as Mia Dolan, whose assistance as a paranormal consultant with the

Soul Rescue: Lost Children in the Dark

 Imagine the plight of a huddle of children, cold, unattended, and shivering with shock as they stare at the desolate rubble of a building they used to call home. It is war; the very air is clogged with gray dust and they are the unfortunate victims of a bombing.

Such ghosts are not only trapped on Earth, but are perpetually experiencing their final emotions of fear and pain at the collateral destruction of their lives. They are even unaware they are physically dead.

PERSISTENT GLOOM

The strength of their terror has closed them to all else; they have existed for decades in distress, unaware that the remains of their home were cleared and new dwellings put up where generations of people had been living. Yet the unchanging despair experienced by the children in their timeless state may be felt by sensitive living, perhaps as a persistent atmosphere of gloom and depression.

In such a case, the usual spirit guides cannot help the children pass into the spirit realms because they are too closed and inward-looking, blinded by their own suffering. Somehow, mercifully, a living medium can reach them.

A CHANGED ENVIRONMENT

One technique used by those who specialize in soul rescue is to clairvoyantly see the ghosts, in this case standing amid the rubble, and subtly change the picture. For instance, the rescuer might concentrate on the piece of ground immediately beneath their feet and change it from debris-strewn pavement to a patch of grass. Instead of gray, it is a vibrant green, and it is soft and pliant in warm sunshine. To help them feel the difference, the ghosts may be visualized as being barefooted. Once they notice their environment has changed, they are on the road to being released.

This introduced landscape can then be developed, showing the ghosts that there is a greater reality than they are experiencing —one in which they have existed since they were frozen by fear. The rescuer shows them caring, compassion, love, and faith in an afterlife of joy and freedom. Once the children can communicate with the rescuer, they are introduced to the spirit guides who have always been ready to take them through the light portal, and they will be finally free. The atmosphere of despondency will have been lifted from the neighborhood and the rescuer will have performed another act of kindness to complete strangers.

Souls That Attach Themselves

Medium Ian Bradley does not suppose that all rescued souls go to the same place. Sometimes a person's soul is not trapped by a place or frozen in a moment, but wanders with some freedom. These souls may attach themselves to people or even animals.

One such ghost of a man attached himself to Ian's pet dog. The man had suffered some learning difficulties and felt more comfortable with dogs than people. Communication, therefore, between soul and rescuer was difficult as the ghost simply didn't believe in Ian's description of a better place that awaited him in the spirit realm.

DIVERTING ATTENTION
Ian tried to take the ghost's attention away from his dog by showing him a charming meadow full of beauty, wild animals, and even a dog. But the ghost's attachment to the real dog was too strong. Then the spirit guides, who were assisting in releasing the ghost from his Earthbound state, brought in the spirit of a dog that Ian's wife had owned before it died.

The emotional attachment between Ian's wife and the spirit dog was so strong that the ghost, who was stubbornly mistrustful of humans, was moved and accepted it as being as real as anything else. With this connection made, the spirit guides and ghost dog led the human ghost away from the mundane world.

GAINING CONFIDENCE
Ian adds that the ghost was not ready to move far into the realm of spirit, but was given a small cottage to live in. It was distant from any neighbors, but had a quiet road at the front. Every so often a gentleman would walk his dog along the road. And little by little the ghost would pluck up the courage to greet the dog and his owner and would gradually gain the confidence to be trusting. Eventually he would be introduced to the wider world of spirit.

UK TV show *Haunted Homes* (2006) successfully cleansed a private house in Nottingham, UK, which had suffered from a brooding sense of oppression and unrest. Her 20-minute cleansing ceremony was described as intense, but was not televized. Two months afterward the inhabitants described the ghost as having left, saying that the children were happy to be in the house, that a weight had been lifted from their shoulders, and that they now felt safe to live there.

Although few mediums specialize in soul rescue, some, such as Ian Bradley (see box above,) are happy to promote it as a vital part of their work. While the complexity of dealing with spirits is too great to detail here, and a little knowledge can be a dangerous thing (similar to thinking that just turning an ignition key is all you need to know in order to drive a car,) the value of the service is not hard to understand.

Natural Amulets

 The origin of the word "amulet" is unknown, but it seems to refer to an object that is worn by, or hung upon something, to protect it.

Some objects may have intrinsic power over us. For example, a blood-red ruby will inspire emotions of an eruptive and passionate nature, while a deep-green emerald will produce a mood of power patiently applied. Using this system we may find allies among the natural world, objects that will support and assist us when we feel threatened by ghosts.

INNER FEAR
The arch wit and American author Ambrose Bierce wrote in his *Devil's Dictionary* that a ghost is actually the outward form of an inner fear. While there may be more to it than that, he certainly has a point. Various exorcists have estimated that at least 80 percent of their case load is not paranormal at all, but is directly due to either mental or physical health problems. Calming such unnecessary fears would obviously leave us better able to cope with the remaining matters.

We have already encountered the Golden Bough (see page 36), which was used to provide safe passage through the Underworld. But there are alternatives that are less of a challenge to obtain.

Ghosts are strongly associated with the night, with the unknown. We can do much to counter our fear of this darkness, by having an amulet associated with the day, with the known, and with the light.

DAYLIGHT
The Sun is the supreme symbol of day and transparent yellow or golden stones are powerful reminders of the beauty and strength of daylight. Citrine is an excellent example and has a tradition of promoting psychic abilities, making it protective and helping us perceive the truth of paranormal phenomena. While some might prefer their citrine to be faceted and mounted in gold (the metal associated with the Sun), a tumble-polished specimen is fine.

The feel of your chosen stone is as important as the look of it, as one popular way to use it is as a worry egg, held in the hand as a tangible reminder of life's positive side. Tiger's eye is a good alternative to citrine. Its chatoyance, or light-play, is said to promote the development of second sight.

Some researchers recommend amber, which is famous for its ability to develop a static electrical charge and attract particles of dust. This natural property inspired the tradition that it also cleanses and purifies in a spiritual way. However, in a haunted site we may not wish to

attract impure energies. And also, given that amber is fossilized sap from a long-dead tree, and some specimens contain body parts of other dead creatures, taking this stone into a haunting situation may be provocative.

NOTES ON SHAPE

While more difficult to find, a polished sphere of citrine makes a powerful amulet, as its shape is not only that of the Sun, but it reminds us of the strength of the three-dimensional magic circle that can surround and protect us. Another traditional protection is an eye stone. These may be found on beaches and are formed from a rock with distinctive layers, which have been eroded so that only a disc of one remains, surrounded by the other. Such natural treasures may be the object of a psychic quest.

ALLIES THAT BOOST GOOD VIBES

With fabulous colors and eye-catching patterns, natural stones and jewelry, even items such as feathers, can help break into a negative mood and switch our thoughts into a positive direction, just by us looking at them.

Banded stones, such as onyx (a form of agate, itself a member of the chalcedony family) and malachite, are often cut and polished to show concentric circles, making beautiful eye stones. Rather like the eyes on butterfly wings that frighten away predators, eye stones distract, weaken, and ward off malevolent spirits.

SYNCHRONICITY

We all experience surprising coincidences. Sometimes they are useful and nudge us into remembering something important. At other times they may seem to purposefully cluster around a particular theme. The psychiatrist Carl Jung (1875–1961) coined the word "synchronicity," togetherness in time, to describe such events and parapsychologists are still building on his groundbreaking work. To many people, synchronicity is a joy, but to others it becomes a burden, yet its negative effects can be managed.

Psychic residue

Paranormal researchers report clusters of bizarre coincidences during or immediately following an investigation. At its most extreme, some people regard it as a form of psychic residue picked up from our encounter with the spirit world; a sort of contamination that needs to be cleansed before normal life can resume. If it persists it may become an obsession, but cases are rare and it usually subsides after a few days or weeks.

Many people who start investigating ghosts find themselves surrounded by synchronicities (see also pages 84–5). This can be upsetting because a synchronicity is only relevant to you, which means that, apparently, the whole world has conspired to give you a message, a nudge. Is the cosmos alive and interacting directly with you?

Coping with synchronicity

Facing up to a question like that is just one of many reasons why it's hard to start investigating the paranormal on your own. It's usually best to find a group with a wide range of views, who can agree to disagree while they conduct their research. This will, at least, provide a balance of ideas, and forestall a hasty decision.

Acceptance

It is often the case that phenomena in a haunted house will subside, and sometimes stop altogether, as soon as the people who live there accept that there is a ghost. Synchronicity often behaves in the same way—when we decide to investigate the subject around which such synchronicities are clustering, they rapidly diminish into comfortable familiarity and vanish. Unfortunately, that does not mean a cluster of similar, or seemingly linked, events can be trusted to guide us into a course of action.

We can easily test the power of the mind and create a sort of synchronicity by using willpower to abstain from something. The forbidden fruit starts cropping up almost immediately. Dieting is a prime example—almost anything can remind us of the one thing we're supposed to be ignoring. Properly handled, this heightened awareness can temper willpower and make it stronger and better able to resist temptation.

The power of love

Love is an extreme manifestation of this dynamic relationship between ourselves and something else. When we're in love, we don't need anything to remind us of our lover. We ourselves are the trigger. Although our loved one may be physically far away, we feel they are never absent, but are an ever-present reality—and this perception can persist even after they suffer bodily death. It may be supposed that true love is synchronicity raised to the power of infinity. When we become sensitized to synchronicities, we may actually become sensitized to synchronicity itself. We may notice it cropping up in other parts of our lives, making connections where we'd least expect them, leading us toward an understanding of the universal nature of spiritual love.

Quantum physicists and astrophysicists approach their studies of the Universe from opposite ends, but both are finding increasingly deep connections between everything they observe. This profound inter-connectivity appears to mirror the mystical perception of a fundamental unity of all things. Synchronicity can sometimes feel like a mystical revelation, a momentary awakening from a grand illusion or universal dream. Even that which seemingly stands apart, is a part of a greater whole.

Four-dimensional pareidolia?
Perhaps, though, we should think twice before allowing ourselves to be seduced by the mystical interpretation of synchronicity. While some people find such coincidences meaningful, many insist they are meaningless. To them, synchronicity is merely four-dimensional pareidolia, a pattern perceived in random events by people yearning to see the face of God.

Our brains are certainly hard-wired to try to make sense out of the chaotic world we inhabit, which may be why we feel compelled to solve mysteries such as synchronicity. And, just as with the

question of whether ghosts are real or illusions, the stakes in the synchronicity debate are high. It goes beyond our relationship with divinity; it questions the structure of reality itself.

SITTING ON THE FENCE
There is a theory that the two reactions to synchronicity (belief and scepticism) are each choreographed by one of the two lobes of the brain. Perhaps, then, the best approach may be to sit on the fence between them and stay on good terms with both neighbors, rather than be lobotomized by either one.

The view from the fence is clear and the grass is green on both sides. We should not be afraid to explore the territories on either side, but whichever way we travel we should always keep our sense of balance. That, and a sense of humor, is our guide to returning safely to the middle ground—where we can all meet up and discuss our experiences.

GROUP WELFARE
One of the benefits of investigating the paranormal as part of a group is that if we feel we've been contaminated or badly affected by contact with a spirit, we can seek and receive help promptly from people we know and trust.

Welfare team
Every investigation group needs a welfare team. In small group, this is likely to be composed of everyone; in larger groups, senior members tend to take on this role. Ideally this team should have a balance between sceptics and believers, and

Achilles

 Giving the body a proper funeral is one of the most common ways of preventing a spirit becoming Earthbound. In the *Iliad* (8th century BCE) Homer gives a vivid account of the grief of the hero Achilles, who mourns the death of Patroclus, who was slain in the Trojan War.

Achilles goes alone to the open shoreline and eventually falls exhausted into a deep sleep. That night the slain man's spirit comes and hovers over him, looking exactly as he had in life. Patroclus begs Achilles to bury him because when his spirit tried to enter the house of Hades, the Underworld, he was driven away. He is doomed to wander endlessly outside its gates as an Earthbound spirit, until his body receives the proper funeral rites.

Achilles tries to embrace his friend, but the spirit vanishes like a mist and, whining, descends into the Earth. The following night, the necessary pyre is lit and Achilles drenches the ground with wine as a libation, dedicating it to Patroclus by name. When the pyre has done its work, a barrow of earth is raised above his bones and the spirit of his friend finds peace in the house of Hades.

people with as wide an experience of life as possible. Naturally, the welfare team must be trusted to treat every case with respect and in strictest confidence. While their services will rarely be called upon, these individuals must be willing to mobilize instantly a problem arises.

OBSESSION

Unlike possession, where the victim seems to undergo a personality change, people suffering from obsession are simply driven to extremes by an idea. The dividing line between obsession and devotion to a cause is a fine one. Much depends on what other opportunities are missed along the way. These needn't be important opportunities. The first signs of an obsession may be as mundane as losing a set of keys, or leaving lights or taps turned on. Such events may even be mistaken as poltergeist activity, but they are really just symptoms of being distracted.

Shared responsibility

Everyone in a paranormal investigation team takes responsibility for keeping its members safe. If anyone shows signs of becoming obsessed with a particular site, spirit, or issue, great care needs to be taken to minimize their suffering. If their goal is attainable, the team must rally round and

Obsessed by Hauntings

 The theme of a man becoming obsessively haunted by the spirit of a murdered young woman is explored in the 2000 movie *Stir of Echoes*, which is set in urban Chicago. Starring Kevin Bacon as Tom Witzky and Kathryn Erbe as his sceptical wife Maggie, the movie charts his descent into mind-shearing obsession. He is willing to sacrifice all to find the reason for the repeated appearances of the ghost of a young woman.

Maggie struggles to cope with Tom's behavior and finds herself touching the scary fringe of a secret society of psychics. But Tom pursues his obsession alone, tearing his family apart as he looks for the corpse. This gripping supernatural drama culminates cleverly in a satisfying revelation of the crime.

Good horror movies, like bad dreams, take frightening situations to extremes. The classic movie *The Haunting* (1963) takes us, with four paranormal investigators, into a malevolent house hidden away in New England. The makeshift team is led by Dr. John Markway (Richard Johnson), who doesn't know that the personal background of one of the women on the team—Eleanor Lance (Julie Harris)—corresponds exactly with part of the history of the haunted house.

Eleanor grows increasingly obsessed with her role there, coming to believe she has a special relationship with the haunting and increasingly feeling she belongs with the house. In the final reel, this conviction becomes a self-fulfilling prophesy.

lighten their burden by sharing the enterprise. By moving the project on to its natural conclusion more quickly, and in good company, the risk of anyone falling prey to a lonely obsession is greatly reduced. By definition, a fully fledged obsession is irrational. More experienced groups may be able to offer some assistance through a team training session. Discussing similar cases and the ways the sufferers coped may be enough to pull a sufferer through. But if there is any doubt

that this may not be sufficient, professional help should be sought at once.

POSSESSION
This is perhaps the greatest fear of anyone becoming involved in paranormal investigation. The feeling of having one's identity forced aside and replaced against our will by alien thoughts is the stuff of nightmares and Hollywood has successfully capitalized on this theme.

The Exorcist

Classic supernatural horror movies such as *The Exorcist* (1973) have established possession in the public imagination as the worst-case scenario for people who dabble with spirits. However, that exorcism had nothing to do with ghosts—it was a case of demonic possession.

Trance mediums

Possession by ghosts is the stock-in-trade of trance mediums, who deliberately allow their minds and bodies to be controlled by the disincarnate spirit. This allows the spirit to communicate in a more natural way. The medium usually has no knowledge of what they are saying or doing, as they are in a trance.

The medium in the 1990 romantic comedy *Ghost* enabled lovers separated by death to reunite briefly by allowing her body to be possessed by the romantic ghost for a final farewell kiss. Earlier in the movie a spontaneous possession is played for laughs. Because of the similarity in symptoms between possession and certain physical and psychological illnesses, anyone who suspects

STIR OF ECHOES, MOVIE

An innocent man struggles with the violent ghost of a murder victim. This cult 1999 movie stars Kevin Bacon as a man driven to obsession by his need to solve the mystery of his ghostly encounters.

The Pentagram

A supremely effective talisman for protection in a situation involving malevolent spirits is the pentagram, or five-pointed star. The usual form is of interlacing lines rather than the solid star used by the military.

The pentagram is all about being in touch with the physical world, which is exactly what we need when something is threatening to scare us, literally, out of our wits. This star is a symbol of ourselves as human beings— four limbs surmounted by the head.

The five points also represent the four elements of fire, air, water, and earth, with the fifth element of spirit at the apex. While both we and the ghost have the fifth element of spirit, the ghost lacks what we plainly have—

a body composed of physical elements. If for no other reason than this, we will always be stronger than a disembodied spirit. The pentagram reminds us of this fact.

The more often and more deeply we focus on the properties of the pentagram, the more we are able to gather its power into ourselves— making our own spirit and body our ultimate natural defence against evil.

they may have been possessed should seek professional help.

PREVENTION, BETTER THAN CURE

Protecting ourselves from ghosts wouldn't be necessary if there weren't any. Sceptics might regard that as self-evident, but believers also support the view. Perhaps the surest way to stop ourselves being bothered by ghosts is to ensure that they do not linger among the living, but are

encouraged to move swiftly on into the Afterlife. Most cultures have their ways of achieving this smooth transition and even in the secular West some of these methods remain in common use. The most frequently observed superstition is opening doors and windows immediately after a death in a house. This shows the ghost that we understand that the time has come for it to leave. Of course, in the case of a long illness, where the invalid has been protected from chilling draughts,

Live Well, Die Well!

Perhaps the single most valuable technique for protecting the living from the ghosts of the dead is something we must each do for ourselves. If we each live our life in such a way that nothing important is left undone and our loved ones all know how much we cherish them, we will not only be able to sleep well at night, but when the time comes, we may die and rest in peace sublime.

A CHRISTMAS CAROL
The classic ghost story *A Christmas Carol* was written by Charles Dickens in 1843 and has become a perennial favorite in book form, on stage, on TV, and in the movies. From the faithful TV version *A Christmas Carol* (1999), starring Patrick Stewart as the infamous Ebenezer Scrooge, to Bill Murray's immortal performance of the role in *Scrooged* (1988), the message from beyond the grave is always crystal clear. When the miserly Scrooge is visited by the dreadful ghost of his business partner Jacob Marley, he is terrified and asks "But why do spirits walk the Earth, and why do they come to me?"

"It is required of every man," the ghost responds, "that the spirit within him should walk abroad among his fellow men and travel far and wide; and if that spirit goes not forth in life, it is condemned to do so after death. It is doomed to wander through the world—oh, woe is me!—and witness what it cannot share, but might have shared on Earth, and turned to happiness!"

opening windows to allow a change of air is also a healthy, practical thing to do. It also reminds the bereaved that there is a world outside, the world of the living, where friends and fresh opportunities await. Some people drape their mirrors, so the ghost cannot become confused by seeing its reflection and remain transfixed in the house. This can also prevent spirits from using the mirrors as a portal to enter and haunt the house.

The idea that the corpse should be carried out of the house feet first, to prevent it returning, is often observed, but is not easy to explain in terms of psychological benefit for the bereaved.

The journey from the living

The ritual of moving all the furniture and ornaments around is supposed to prevent the ghost from remaining in familiar and comfortable surroundings, where it may settle down with ease. The disruption in its surroundings is supposed to encourage it to commence its proper journey away from the living, into the realm of spirit. It also gives the bereaved a clean break with the past, so they can create a new future.

40 Great Ghost Stories

Ghosts and hauntings have always been the subjects of stories and novels. Here are 40 of the best to look out for:

- *Ghosts: Another Summer in the Old Town*, Randy Cribbs, 2009
- *The Book of Illumination*, Mary Anne Winkowski, 2009
- *The Little Stranger*, Sarah Waters, 2009
- *A Frightful Move*, Chris Varga, 2008
- *Ghost of a Chance*, Katie MacAlister, 2008
- *Ghost Whisperer: Revenge*, Doranna Durgin, 2008
- *The Graveyard Book*, Neil Gaiman, 2008
- *Ghost, Interrupted*, Sonia Singh, 2007
- *Heart-shaped Box*, Joe Hill, 2007
- *The Ghost of Mary Prairie*, Lisa Polisar, 2007
- *The Hangin' Oak*, D.L. Havlin, 2006
- *The Lissergool Ghost*, Mollie Sharkey-Wilmot, 2005
- *Blithe Spirit*, Noel Coward (adapted by Charles Osborne), 2004
- *Pharos: A Ghost Story*, Alice Thompson, 2002
- *The Complete Wandering Ghosts*, F. Marion Crawford, 2002
- *The Ghost of Harmony Hall*, Lawrence J. Hogan, 2002
- *The Diary of Ellen Rimbauer: My Life at Rose Red*, Ridley Pearson, 2001
- *Shadowland (The Mediator, Book 1)*, Meg Cabot, 2000

- *Women and Ghosts*, Alison Lurie, 1995
- *Ghost Singer*, Anna Lee Walters, 1994
- *Ghosts*, Noel Hynd, 1993
- *Julian's House*, Judith Hawkes, 1990
- *High Spirits: A Collection of Ghost Stories*, Robertson Davies, 1982
- *The Shining*, Stephen King, 1977
- *Best Ghost Stories*, Algernon Blackwood, 1973
- *Hell House*, Richard Matheson, 1971
- *The Haunting of Hill House*, Shirley Jackson, 1959
- *Poor Girl*, Elizabeth Taylor, 1955
- *Who is Sylvia?*, Cynthia Asquith, 1955
- *Tales of Horror and the Supernatural*, Arthur Machen, 1948
- *The Ghost and Mrs. Muir*, R.A. Dick, 1945
- *Carnacki the Ghost-Finder*, William Hope Hodgson, 1913
- *The Moonlit Road*, Ambrose Bierce, 1907
- *Ghost Stories of an Antiquary*, M.R. James, 1904
- *Kwaidan: Stories and Studies of Strange Things*, Lafcadio Hearn, 1903
- *The Turn of the Screw*, Henry James, 1898
- *The Canterville Ghost*, Oscar Wilde, 1887
- *Dickon the Devil*, J.S. LeFanu, 1871
- *A Christmas Carol*, Charles Dickens, 1843
- *Hamlet*, William Shakespeare, 1599

Actress Ingrid Bergman with child actor Heywood Morse in scene from The Turn of the Screw.

Glossary

Apophenia The perception of meaningful connections where none exist. This is an umbrella term that includes more specific examples such as pareidolia and synchronicity.

Arrival apparition The ghost of a living person, and it may be similar to a crisis apparition (although it is usually less communicative.) Such phenomena are usually encountered where the person is shortly to arrive (whether they are expected or not.)

Calling out A procedure sometimes employed during a seance, where the spirits are literally spoken to, out loud, usually with an invitation to communicate with the participants. This might as easily attract hostile spirits as benign ones, making it controversial, and some people regard it as positively dangerous.

Clairvoyance The (alleged) ability to be able to see things that are beyond the normal range of the senses.

Crisis apparition At an instant of ultimate crisis in a person's life, most frequently the moment of death, that person might appear to a friend or loved one, usually to give them a farewell message. This may be a true ghost, involving the spirit of the person, but some people suggest that it is actually a case of telepathy. See also Arrival apparition.

EIF Experience-Inducing Fields are magnetic fields that affect the brain, causing a form of hallucination. EIFs may occur naturally, for example during earthquakes, and are increasingly common in our man-made environment, where they may be generated by some industrial and domestic electric appliances.

ESP Extra-Sensory Perception is the ability to know something without using the physical senses such as touch, sight, or hearing. Increasingly sophisticated experiments designed by parapsychologists are testing the nature of this so-called sixth sense, but despite some interesting findings, its existence remains controversial.

EVP Electronic Voice Phenomena are recordings of sounds that appear to have been produced paranormally. Frequent examples are seemingly whispered words that were recorded despite nothing being heard by the people who were making the recording.

Genius loci Literally the spirit of the place. Usually a personification of an exceptionally beautiful or impressive natural site. Some sensitive people describe their visions, which tend to resemble deities rather than ghosts, in detail, but at other times these spirits appear spontaneously as vague figures in a landscape, and are assumed to be ghosts.

Ghost Astonishingly, this word is impossible to define succinctly as it has come to mean different things to different people. It is usually read as meaning the disincarnate spirit of a person whose body is dead, but people also report sightings of ghosts of animals, objects (stone-tape ghosts), places (genius loci), and even of living people (crisis apparitions.)

Haunted A place, object, or person that is frequently attended by phenomena linked with ghosts or other spirits.

Mahatma A Sanskrit word meaning "great soul." It is a title given to someone who has evolved beyond their own ego with its selfish needs and desires, and has become mindful of the rights and liberties of others—all others.

Necromancy The art of calling up the dead, especially to gain information about the future.

Orb A translucent disc of light in a photograph or video. These are usually caused by dust close to the camera and out of focus, brightly illuminated by the camera flash. Before this mundane cause was known about, many people believed orbs were paranormal.

Ouija board This well-known type of talking board is trademarked (Parker Brothers), but the name is often used generically. It may involve using a planchette or pointer that slides toward numbers and letters to spell out a message. Marketed as a game, it may sound simple and safe, but some people regard this device as potentially dangerous because the users tend to call out and may attract malevolent spirits.

Pareidolia The perception of a meaningful image in a random picture or sound. Examples include seeing the "man in the Moon," and hearing the sound of a telephone ringing while taking a shower. It is a form of apophenia.

Planchette This is a tablet large enough for several people to put their fingers on, which is mounted on bearings that enable it to be moved freely across a tabletop. A piece of paper is placed beneath it and a pen is mounted in the center, so that when the planchette moves it draws pictures or writes words. This tool attracts the same controversy as calling out. See also Ouija board.

Poltergeist This is more than just a "noisy ghost" and it may not be a spirit at all. Most physical effects, such as moving objects around, are credited to poltergeists, but studies suggest that the power behind this phenomena is often a living person. Hoaxes are not uncommon.

Primed expectation This is a powerful psychological factor that makes us tend to see what we expect to see. Combined with peer pressure (the desire to fit in with our companions) we may be swept along in a scenario that, in its extreme form, could be called mass hypnosis.

Psychic quest The idea of a quest is to find or achieve something of value, and a psychic quest places the object in the realm of spirit or mind. The goal may be a spiritual revelation, such as seeing your first ghost, self discovery, or helping a spirit find peace. Clues may be found anywhere, such as in dreams, synchronicities, or in the comments of companions, yet their importance may not be at once apparent.

Psychometry The word was coined in 1842 by American professor Joseph Rhodes Buchanan from words meaning "soul" and "measure"— combining to describe the supposed ability of the human soul to be aware of things beyond the reach of the physical senses. As a form of ESP (see above) it is often used to investigate haunted houses, and may be related to stone-tape ghosts.

Residual energy Just as ripples, echoes, and aftershocks follow certain physical events, powerful spiritual events are said to leave traces that linger through time. While these may be sensed, and even affect people in the present day, this sort of ghost is essentially unconscious and inert. See Stone tape.

Seance A meeting at which people attempt to communicate with the spirits of the departed. The services of a medium, or apparatus such as a talking board, may be used, but are not essential. The word derives from the French *séance*, meaning "sitting."

Spirit Many paranormal researchers claim ghosts are not spirits, while others see no distinction. A haunting in which somebody encounters a ghost may be explained by natural science, but a spirit is supernatural. A spirit need not be the soul of a person; it could be an angel or demon, an elemental, or a deity. The spirit world could theoretically permeate all matter and extend into other dimensions and realms beyond.

Stone tape Referring to magnetic tape used to record sound and video, this idea suggests that stone and other elements in the environment can somehow record events. These recordings may be replayed, giving us a faithful glimpse of the past. Stone-tape ghosts cannot interact, making them relatively safe to study.

Synchronicity A term coined by the psychologist C.G. Jung to denote a connection sensed between events that are not linked by cause and

effect but by the coincidence of their timing. While many people regard synchronicity as a figment of the imagination, others use it as a sort of spiritual guide.

Talking board Any smooth surface that has the letters of the alphabet and numerals positioned so that a moveable pointer may indicate them one at a time. Spirits may animate the pointer (usually through people who are touching it) to spell out messages. See Ouija board.

Theosophy Literally "God wisdom," theosophy is one of the more influential of many occult movements to study the spirit's place in the Universe. Founded in 1875 in New York, the Theosophical Society promotes research into occultism and comparative religion and endorses liberation from discrimination by race, gender, creed, or caste.

Trance mediumship Probably the most inherently dangerous of all psychic phenomena. The medium allows the spirit to enter and inhabit their body, to speak and do as it wishes. The medium is rarely aware of anything that happens during the trance. This form of mediumship is usually only attempted after many years of study, and with the assistance of a trusted spirit guide.

Trigger objects These are items brought into a haunted environment in the hope of prompting—triggering—a manifestation. The items are carefully positioned so that any movement can be detected. They may be particularly useful in poltergeist situations.

Vardoger See Arrival apparition.

Vigil A period of time devoted to communicating with ghosts, traditionally during the hours normally given over to sleep. A vigil may be undertaken alone or in a group, and may include a wide range of activities, or simply just sitting in silence.

Zombie This is really the opposite of a ghost—it is the body without a human spirit, vivified by the will of another person, who controls its every act.

Bibliography

Anon., *CNN Larry King Live*, Atlanta (Georgia), Cable News Network, http://transcripts.cnn.com

Anon., *File No: 09-10-021*, The Pennsylvania Paranormal Association, www.theppa.net

Anon., *History of the Talking Board*, Museum of Talking Boards, www.museumoftalkingboards.com

Anon., *Mr. Haggard's Strange Dream*, The New York Times, 31 July 1904

Anon., *Ofcom broadcast bulletin,* issue number 49, 5 December 2005, London, Ofcom, www.ofcom.org.uk

Anon., *Police probed claims by psychics*, London, BBC, http://news.bbc.co.uk

Anon., *The George Inn Blackawton*, Hidden Realms, www.hiddenrealms.org.uk

Betzger, Bruce M. and Michael D. Coogan (eds.), *The Oxford Companion to the Bible*, Oxford, Oxford University Press, 1993

Bierce, Ambrose, *The Devil's Dictionary*, New York, Dover Publications, 1958

Brown, David, *Madeleine police use psychic reports in hunt for girl*, London, *Times Newspapers*, www.timesonline.co.uk

Coleman, Graham (ed.), *The Tibetan Book of the Dead*, London, Penguin Classics, 2005

Collyer, Graham, *Exercise tiger victim puts in an anniversary "appearance,"* Dartmouth Chronicle, 23 May 2008

Coogan, Michael D., Marc Z. Brettler, Carol A. Newsom, Pheme Perkins (eds.), *The New Oxford Annotated Bible, New Revised Standard Version with the Apocrypha*, Oxford, Oxford University Press, 2007

Crowley, Aleister (ed.), *The Goetia*, York Beach (Maine), Samuel Weiser, 1995

Dickens, Charles, *A Christmas Carol*, London, Chapman & Hall, 1843

Doniger, Wendy, *The Rig Veda*, London, Penguin Classics, 2003

Evans, Roger, *Somerset Stories of the Supernatural*, Newbury, Countryside Books, 2001

Forman, Joan, *The Haunted South*, Norwich, Jarrold Colour Publications, 1989

George, Andrew, *The Epic of Gilgamesh*, Harmondsworth, Allen Lane, 1999

Goethe (trans. John Oxenford), *The Autobiography of Goethe*, London, Henry G. Bohn, 1848

Grinnell, George Bird, *Pawnee Hero Stories and Folk-Tales*, Lincoln (Nebraska), University of Nebraska Press, 1961

Hammon, Peter J., *Sapphire and Steel*, London, Star, 1979

Harper, Charles G., *The Ingoldsby Country*, London, Adam & Charles Black, 1904

Hippisley, John, *Ghost Tour*, The Canterbury Ghost Tour, www.canterburyghosttour.com

Hippisley, John, *Haunted Canterbury*, Stroud, The History Press, 2009

Hole, Christina, *Haunted England*, London, Batsford, 1941

Homer (trans. E. V. Rieu), *The Iliad*, London, Penguin Classics, 2003

Homer (trans. E. V. Rieu), *The Odyssey*, London, Penguin Classics, 2003

Hutton, Ronald, *The Stations of the Sun*, Oxford, Oxford University Press, 1996

Huxley, Aldous, *Island*, London, Vintage Classics, 2008

Inman, Vanda, *St. Clether Holy Well Chapel*, St. Clether Holy Well Chapel, www.peaceland.org.uk

Jackson, Kenneth Hurlstone, *A Celtic Miscellany*, Harmondsworth, Penguin Books, 1971

Johnson, E. Pauline (Tekahionwake), *Legends of Vancouver*, Vancouver, Pauline Johnson Trust, 1911

Jung, C.G., *Memories, Dreams, Reflections*, London, Collins and Routledge, 1963

Lamont-Brown, Raymond, *Scottish Folklore*, Edinburgh, Birlinn, 1996

Lévi, Eliphas (trans. A. E. Waite), *Transcendental Magic*, London, Redway, 1896

Mann, Bob, *The Ghosts of Totnes*, Exeter, Obelisk Publications, 1993

Martin, Andrew, *Ghoul Britannia*, London, Short Books, 2009

McLaughlin, Marie L., *Myths and Legends of the Sioux*, Bismarck (North Dakota), Bismarck Tribune Co., 1916

Muir, Hazel, *Where do ghosts come from?*, New Scientist, issue 2732, 30 October 2009

Mutwa, Vusamazulu Credo, *Indaba My Children: African Folktales*, New York, Grove Press, 1999

O'Donnell, Elliott, *Scottish Ghost Stories*, Teddington, Echo Library, 2007

Persinger, Michael, *Neuropsychological Bases of God Beliefs*, New York, Praeger Publishers, 1987

Plato (trans. Walter Hamilton), *Gorgias*, London, Penguin Classics, 2004

Power, Joe, *Police Investigations*, Joe Power, www.joepower.co.uk

Power, Joe, *The Man Who Sees Dead People*, London, Penguin, 2009

Sleight, Kate, *Chambers Ghosts and Spirits*, Edinburgh, Chambers, 2008

Spencer, John and Tony Wells, *Ghost Watching*, London, Virgin, 1995

Tancred, George, *Rulewater and its People*, Edinburgh, T. & A. Constable, 1907

Taylor, Ken, *Brislington Ghosts and Mysteries*, Bristol, Redcliffe Press, 2005

Taylor, Ken, *Dartmouth Ghosts and Mysteries*, Dartmouth, Richard Webb, 2006

Taylor, Ken, *Ghosts of Arnos Manor Hotel, Bristol*, Bristol, Archyve, 2009

Taylor, Troy, *Spirits of the Civil War Gettysburg*, Troy Taylor and Whitechapel Productions Press, www.prairieghosts.com

Townsend, Maurice, *Magnetic Hallucinations*, www.assap.org

Twain, Mark, *How to Tell a Story and Other Essays*, Oxford University Press, 1996

Underwood, Peter, *The A–Z of British Ghosts*, London, Souvenir Press, 1971

Virgil (trans. David West), *The Aeneid*, London, Penguin Classics, 2003

Zontok, John, *The Man in Overalls—Barkhamsted, CT*, Northwest Connecticut Paranormal Society, www.northwestconnecticutparanormal.com

Further Reading

NON-FICTION

Austin, Joanne, *Weird Hauntings*, New York, Sterling, 2006
A hefty catalog of America's ghost stories. This selection has been compiled for thrills and contains the scariest tales the author could find. Haunted locations include private and public sites.

Butler, Walter Ernest, *How to Develop Psychometry*, London, Aquarian Press, 1971
One of several practical guides written by Butler (1898–1978) dealing with various aspects of clairvoyance and magic. Butler trained as a medium, studied theosophy, and practiced mysticism in India, before founding the Servants of the Light in 1965, which is a modern mystery school teaching esoteric arts using the Qabalah.

Fontana, David, *Is There an Afterlife?*, Oakland (California), O Books, 2005
This book uses both science and religion to look into the question of what part of ourselves might survive physical death, discusses theories about the nature of the Afterlife, and tackles the ethical questions raised by the issues.

Guiley, Rosemary, *The Encyclopedia of Ghosts and Spirits*, New York, Checkmark Books, 2007
This updated version (3rd edition) contains over 600 entries. Written in an engaging style, this book aims to be the definitive work on the subject.

Horn, Stacy, *Unbelievable*, New York, Ecco, 2009
An unbiased account of investigations by the Duke Parapsychology Laboratory into ghosts and poltergeists as well as other paranormal phenomena. Includes follow-ups on some of the cases researched by the famous center run by J. B. Rhine.

Marrs, Jim, *PSI Spies*, Franklin Lakes (New Jersey), Career Press, 2007
An account of the US Army's formerly top-secret remote-viewing program that explored the practical issues of psychic warfare.

McCloy, Nicola, *Sensing Murder*, Auckland (New Zealand), Hodder Moa, 2008
As well as providing a behind-the-camera look at the filming of ten cases from the chart-topping TV series, this book offers information not previously aired, and also details what happened after screening. Profiles of the four psychics featured on the show are also included.

FICTION

Dante, *Divine Comedy*, widely available in the public domain
A comprehensive and graphic description of what faces the soul after bodily death, seen through the eyes of a Christian of the early 14th century.

Ingoldsby, Thomas, *The Ingoldsby Legends*, widely available in the public domain
A compendium of stories and poems from the 1830s and '40s, many involving ghosts and other supernatural themes. Witty, clever, and humorous (although some tales may offend due their expression of characters in caricature,) these were immensely popular in Victorian England.

James, Henry, *The Turn of the Screw*, widely available in the public domain
First published in 1898, this tells of a young Victorian governess in England who is put in charge of two children and their country mansion. She comes to believe the place is haunted and the children possessed by ghosts of a young couple who have wild and wanton ways. This has been adapted for stage and screen many times.

James, M. R., *Count Magnus and Other Ghost Stories*, London, Penguin Classics, 2006
This complete collection has been claimed to represent the culmination of the 19th-century ghost story tradition in Britain.

Jackson, Shirley, *The Haunting of Hill House*, London, Penguin Classics, 2006
This classic supernatural thriller is hailed as one of the best ghost stories of the 20th century. It was first published in 1959 and has been adapted for the screen in 1963 and 1999, both times under the title *The Haunting*.

WEBSITES

www.aaevp.com
The American Association of Electronic Voice Phenomena (AA-EVP) is dedicated to investigating EVP, and the website offers a wide variety of examples, as well as articles considering the many issues raised.

www.assap.org
The Association for the Scientific Study of Anomalous Phenomena (ASSAP) is a charity devoted to paranormal research and education. It has been investigating a wide range of anomalous phenomena since 1981, with ghosts as a particular specialization, and has a wealth of detailed articles online.

www.csicop.org
The Committee for Skeptical Inquiry is relentless in its efforts to expose the techniques that fraudulent mediums could use to trick and bamboozle their victims, and offers rational explanations for apparently credible claims of paranormal ability.

www.paranormaldatabase.com
Nearly a hundred of the well-known battle ghosts from every period of British history since the Iron Age are listed here.

www.p-s-i.org.uk
Paranormal Site Investigators (PSI) employs the scientific method both to approach investigations and analyze results, and its now recognized as one of the leading paranormal research groups dedicated to onsite investigations.

www.psychicalresearchfoundation.com
The Psychical Research Foundation (PRF) was founded in the US in 1960 as a spin-off from the Rhine Research Center (www.rhine.org), and their website offers a valuable selection of published papers on aspects of the possible continuation of personality and consciousness after physical death.

www.spiritrescue.co.uk
Spirit Rescue and Clearance is a modest but evocative website by Ian Bradley devoted to the vocation of assisting trapped spirits to find release.

www.spr.ac.uk
The Society for Psychical Research was founded in London, UK, in 1882 and is still active in promoting research both by individuals and through university courses in parapsychology.

www.theorbzone.com
The Orb Zone is a free resource devoted to the scientific understanding of orbs. This website is managed by PSI (see www.p-s-i.org.uk above).

Index

Page numbers in *italics* indicate illustrations and captions.

A

acceptance 170
Acheron, River 35
Acorah, Derek 82, 156
Aeacus 35
Aeneid 36
Afterlife 17, 32–7, 38, 40–2, 46–9
  beliefs in 53
Afterlife (TV) 154
Akashic Record 64
Alfriston, Sussex, UK 61
alien abduction 17
All Saints (All Hallows) 42, 44
All Souls 42, 44, 46
Alzheimer's disease 51
American Civil War 59
Amityville, Long Island 114
Amityville Horror (movie) 22, 114
amulets 168–9
ancestor worship 41
angels 13, 22–3
  guardian *22, 23*
animals 108
  ghosts of 61, 62
  souls attached to 167
Antietam, Battle of 59
apophenia 180
apport 107
Arnos Manor Hotel, Bristol, UK 129
arrival apparitions 13, 21, 65, 180
Asphodel Meadow 35
Assaf, Carlos 86
astral body 14
astral planes 14

B

automatic writing 106, *134,* 135
Avebury Stone Circle 60
Aztecs 46–8

Bachelor's Grove Cemetery 114
Bagans, Zak 153
Balder's Dream 100
Bantu religion 41
Barham, Reverend Richard Harris 126–7
battlefields 56–9
Beetlejuice (movie) 110, *110*
Being Human (TV) 154
beliefs 160
"Belmez's faces" *145*
Bible, ghosts in 40–2
Bierce, Ambrose 168
Black Magic 96
blacksmith's ghost 101
Blithe Spirit (movie) *95*
Bloody Mary 114
Boer War *57*
Boleyn, Anne 72
bones, human 48
Book of the Dead 32, *33*
Borley Rectory, Essex, UK 114, *115*
Bradley, Ian 167
brain, limbic system 51
Braithwaite, Jason 52
Brigida 28, *29*
Buchanan, Joseph Rhodes 182

C

calling out 132, 180
cameras 122–4
  problems with 149

Campbell, Laurie 88
Canterbury Cathedral 126–7
cat, invisible 61
Celtic legends 45
Chamberlain, Joseph *57*
Charon *34,* 35, 36
children, rescuing souls of 166
China, Festival of Hungry Souls 165
  Tomb-sweeping Day 48, *49,* 165
Christianity 42, 160, 162
Christmas Carol 177
clairvoyance 70, 76, 180
cleansing 162
coincidences 84–5, 170
coins, in mouth of dead 35
consciousness, quest for 52–3
Coquhonnie Hotel, Strathdon, Scotland 111
Coronado, Pam 88
Cox, Stephen 129, *129*
Craig-y-Nos Castle, Wales 109
crisis apparitions 13, 20, 180
cross 160
Cruikshank, Kelvin 88
Cummins, Geraldine *134*

D

D-Day rehearsals 84–5
Dante Alighieri 42
Dante's Inferno (movie) *43*
Day of the Dead 46–9, *47*
daydreaming 17
De Sarak, Dr. *15*
dead, raising 96–101
death, superstitions 176–7
delusion 13
demons 13, 22, 24, 110

evoking 98
Descartes, René 53
divination 96
Divine Comedy 42
dog, ghost of 62
  soul attached to 167
Dolan, Mia 165–7
Donalgowerie House, Perth,
  Scotland 112–13
Donnelly, Christine 28–9, 84–5
Dostoevsky, Fyodor 50
dowsing 105–7
dreams, significance of 14
dualism 50
DuBois, Allison 82, 89

E
earth mysteries 13
echoes 13, 56
ectoplasm 77, *77*, *79*
Edinburgh Vaults 153
Edward, John 76, 82
Egypt, Ancient 32–5
EIF (Experience-Inducing Fields)
  51–2, 180
Electronic Voice Phenomena *see*
  EVP
Elysian Fields (Elysium) 36, 37
EMF meters 51, 125
Enas 41
Endor, Witch of 82, 96
environment, monitoring 124
epilepsy 50, 51
Epworth House, Lincolnshire, UK
  114
equipment 122–5, 137
ESP (Extra-Sensory Perception) 70,
  180

EVP (Electronic Voice Phenomena)
  108, 135–7, 141, 180–1
exorcism 162
Exorcist (movie) 174
Experience-Inducing Fields *see* EIF
Extra-Sensory Perception *see* ESP

F
fairies 13
Festival of Hungry Souls 165
Fielding, Yvette 140, 152, 156
"Flight 401," Florida 114
Fox sisters 76, 77, 78, 82
fraud 78–80
Fry, Colin 76–7, 82, *83*
funerals 172
Fuseli, Henry *17*

G
genius loci 29, 181
George Inn, Blackawton, Devon, UK
  102–7, *104*
Gettysburg, Pennsylvania 59
Ghost Adventurers (TV) 153
ghost detectors 118
Ghost Hunters (TV) 118, *119*
ghost-hunting 118–57
  analyzing results 142–7
  armchair 152–5
  checklist 120
  experiments 132–41
  famous people 140
  gadgets 122–5, *123*
  preparations 120–1
  site history 120–1
  site report 121
  verifying findings 141
Ghost (movie) 90, *91*, 174

ghost stories, earliest 30–1
  great 94, 178–9
Ghost Whisperer (TV) 81, *81*, 154
Ghostbusters (movie) 160, *161*
ghosts, benevolent 23
  in *Bible* 40–2
  communicating with 76–7,
    96–101
  defense against 160–77
  Earthbound 162
  groups 12–13
  malevolent 22
  meaning of 181
  protection from 160–77
  realm of 12–13
  repeated appearances 56–61, 63
  science of 50–3
  spirits and 28–9
Gilgamesh 30, *31*
God Helmet 50–1
gods and goddesses 13, 29
Goethe, Johann von 65
Golden Bough 36, 168
grave goods 32, 40
Greece, Ancient 35
Gregory IV, Pope 44
grounding 130–1
group welfare 171–2

H
Hades 35
Haggard, Henry Rider 20
Hallowe'en 44–5, *45*
hallucinations 13, 147
Happy Hunting Grounds 92–3
Hardknott Fort, Cumbria, UK 58
Hastings, Battle of 58
Haunted Homes (TV) 167

Haunted (movie) 144
Haunted (TV) 108
Haunting in Connecticut (movie) 22, 26, *27*
Haunting (movie) 24, 173
hauntings 13, 102–15
  imprinted 56–61, 63
  residual 63
Hawes, Jason *119*, 140
Haynes, Professor John-Dylan 53
heart, weighing 32–5, *33*
Heaven 42
Hel (goddess) 100
Hell 42
Hell Bank Money 48, 165
Hidden Realms 102–4, 106, 107
Hinduism 38
hoaxes 13
Holland, John 82
Home, Daniel Douglas 78
Homer 96, 172
  Odyssey 35, 97
Houdini, Harry 78, *79*, 140
human spirit 14–21
Hungry Ghosts, Festival of 48
Huxley, Aldous 50
hypnagogic state 20

I
Iliad 172
incarnations, chain of 40
India 38
individuality 52–3
infrasound 148
Ingoldsby Legends 126–7
Iona, Island of 58
Islands of the Blessed 37

J K
jack-o'-lanterns *45*
Joan of Arc 50
journal 122

Jung, Carl 60, 170, 182
karma 37
Killiecrankie, Battle of 58
Kneale, Nigel 63, *67*

L
Lethbridge, Thomas Charles 63
Lethe, River 36
Lévi, Eliphas 98–101
light, going into 162, 164–5
limbic system 51
Lincoln, Abraham 72
living, ghosts of 13
  protecting 160–77
  way of life 177
location-based ghosts 13
Lodge, Dawn 106
Lost Souls (movie) *163*
love, power of 170–1
lovers, reunited 40
lucid dreaming 14
lunar phases 40

M
McCann, Madeleine 86
magic 63, 68
Mahabharata 39
mahatma 181
Man Who Sees Dead People 87
Marathon, Battle of 56
Matthews, Shannon 87
meditation 160
Medium (TV) *88*, 89, 154
mediums 76–81, 174–6
  abilities 80
  fraud 78–80
  top ten 82
  trance 174–6, 183
Mexico, Day of the Dead 46–9, *47*
Mictecacihuatl 46–8
Mictlan 46

Mictlantcuhtli (Lord of the Dead) 46, 48
mind-body-spirit movement 50
Minos 35
Mnemosyne, pool of 36
Morgan, Sally 92
Moses 50
Most Haunted (TV) 152, *152*, 156–7
movies, horror 110
Muir, Hazel 52
Muncaster Castle, UK 52
murders, investigating 86–8
Murmur (demon) 98, *98*
Mutwa, Vusamazulu Credo 41
Myrtles Plantation, Louisiana 114–15

N
Native Americans 92–3
nature 40
nature spirits 28
near-death experience 18
Nechtansmere, Battle of 58
necromancy 96, 181
new-house syndrome 148–9
Nicholson, Sue 88
nightmares *16*, 17
Niven, David *19*

O
obsession 172–3
Odin 100
Odyssey 35, 97
O'Keeffe, Ciarán 86, 140, 156
Oliver, Edith 60
orbs 151, 181
Orphic mystery 36
Osiris 32, 35
The Others (movie) 162–4
Ouija board 138–9, *139*, 181
out-of-body experience *15*

P Q

Paranormal Activity (movie) 22, 24, *25*
parapsychology 76–85
pareidolia 141, 144–7, 171, 181
Paul, St. 50
Pausanias 56
pentagram 100–1, 160, 176
Persephone 35
Persinger, Dr. Michael A. 50, 52
pets 61–2
Philip, Toronto 115
photographs 128, 132, *133*, *136*, *145*, *146*
  anomalies 151
  double exposure 149, *150*
  flash 151
  misleading 149
pineal gland 53
pipers 111, 112–13
PK *see* psychokinesis
planchette 137, 181–2
police investigations 86–9
Poltergeist (movie) *164*, 165
poltergeists 13, 76, 102–4, *103*, 107, 110–11, 182
possession 110, 162, 173–6
Power, Joe 87
prayer 160, 162
precognition 17
presence 23
Price, Harry 140, *141*
primed expectation 182
protection 160–77
Pseudomonarchia Daemonium 98
psychic art 106, *106*, 129, *129*
psychic investigators 86–9
psychic quests 72, 182
psychokinesis (PK) 76, 102
psychometry 70–3, 107, 132, 182
  experiment in 71
Pure Brightness, Festival of 48

Purgatory 42, 44
Pyramid Texts 32
Quy, Lynsey 87

R

Ragans, Zak 140
Randall and Hopkirk (Deceased) (TV) 89, 154, *155*
Randi, James 78, 140
reincarnation 37–40
religions, comparative 44–5
  wars over 53
religious experiences 51
residual energy 182
"residual" energy hauntings 13
resurrection 42
revenant 13
Rhadamanthus 35
Rig Veda 38
Roman Catholicism 42, 46, 162
Romans 36
Roses, Wars of the 58
Royal Castle Hotel, Dartmouth, UK 147
RSPK (recurrent spontaneous psychokinesis) 102

S

St. Albans, UK 58
St. Clether, Cornwall, UK 28–9, *28*
Samhain 44–5
Samuel (prophet) 42
Sapphire and Steel (TV) 65, *67*, 154
science 50–3
Scooby Doo (TV) 154–5
Sea of Souls (TV) 155
seances 77–8, 182
Segemoor, Battle of 58
Sensing Murder (TV) 88
Seymour, Jane 18
shadows 13, 147
shamans 68

Sheol 40
sites, history 120–1
  report on 121
  securing 134–5
Sixth Sense (movie) 164
Sixth Sense (TV) 76, 82
sketches 132
Slapton Sands 84–5
sleep paralysis 17
smudging 162
Snedeker family 26
Socrates 35
soul mates 40
souls 14
  attaching to person or animal 167
  of children 166
  judgment of 42
  multiple 41
  old 32–42
  rescuing 165–7
  two-tier system 42
  weighing 32–5, *33*
sound-recording equipment 124
Spells for Coming Forth by Day 32
spirit guides 23
spirit level 125
spirits 182
  Earthbound 162, 172
  ghosts and 28–9
  pure 13
  realm of 12
spiritualism 76–8
Stairway to Heaven (movie) 17, *19*
Stavrinou, Jacqui 20
Stir of Echoes (movie) 173, *174–5*
Stockwell, Tony 107
Stokes, Doris 82
stone tape 13, 63, 73, 182
Stone Tape (play) 63, *66*
stones (amulets) 168–9, *169*
Styx, River *34*, 36
Sun 40, 168

Supernatural (TV) 155
superstitions 176–7
synchronicity 170–1, 182–3

T

talismans 68, *69*
talking board 183
Tartarus 35, 36
Taylor, Kai 21
Taylor, Troy 140
telepathy 76
theosophy 183
thoughts, attracting ghosts 160
time travel 17
Tomb-sweeping Day 48, *49*, 165
Topper (TV) 155
Totnes, Devon, UK 101
Tower of London 115
trance mediumship 174–6, 183
trance states 14

trick or treat 44, *45*
trigger objects 134, 183
Turn of the Screw (movie) *179*
TV shows 65, *67*, 76, 81, *81*, 82, 88, *89*, 108, 118, *119*, 152–7
Twain, Mark 21

U V

Underwood, Peter 140
Underworld 32, 35–6, 46
    visit to 30–1
vardoger see arrival apparitions
Vedas 38
Vibes (movie) 72, *73*
vigil 128, 183
    analyzing results 142–7
    false positives 142–4
    preparing for 120–1
Virgil 36
visions 17

W

Webber, Deb 88
Wells, David 82
Weyer, Johann 98
Wiccans 160
willpower 170
Wilson, Grant *119*
Winchester Mystery House 115
witch doctors 41
Witch of Endor 82, 96
Wood, Dave 140
writing, automatic 106, *134*, 135

Y Z

Yama 38, *39*
zombie 183
Zontok, John and Mandi 108

PICTURE CREDITS

akg-images Dimension Films/Album 158; Two Cities/Cineguild/Album 95; **Alamy** Archives du 7eme Art 163; Dale O'Dell 116, 133, 136; **Mary Evans Picture Library** 10, 16, 22, 39, 79, 99, 103; Mr. Edd's Images 146; **Photos 12** 7; Terry Donnelly 45; **BBC Photo Library** 66; **Bridgeman Art Library** Private Collection/Look and Learn 54; Hazel Brown 29; Kim Chatwin 106 above; **Corbis** Earl & Nazima Kowall 49; epa 145; John Springer Collection 43; Momatiuk – Eastcott 131; Roger De La Harpe/Gallo Images 69; Stephen Cox 129 below left; Chris Donnelly 28, 104; **Getty Images** CBS Photo Archive 88; Gordon Parks/Time & Life Images 179; Hulton Archive 19; Spike Mafford 47; Wallace Kirkland 139; Dawn Lodge 106 below; **Mary Evans Picture Library** 15, 34, 74, 143; Harry Price 70, 123; Peter Underwood 141; SPR 77, 134; **Photos12** Ann Ronan Picture Library 57; Archives du 7eme Art 73, 91, 110, 161, 164, 174; Collection Cinema 2; Picture Desk Art Archive/Francesco Venturi 62; Kobal Collection/Blumhouse Productions 25; **The Art Archive/**Archaeological Museum, Aleppo, Syria/Gianni Dagli Orti 31; The Art Archive/British Museum/Jacqueline Hyde 33; The Art Archive/John Meek 61; **Rex Features** Everett Collection 81; ITV 67, 155; Lions Gate/Everett 27, Sci-Fi/Everett 119; Joules Taylor 41, 169; Kai Taylor 98, 129 below right, 176; Ken Taylor 129 above; **TopFoto.co.uk** 83, 150, 152; Fortean 115